House of Heart and HeartBreak

A Family's Struggle With a Daughter's Mental Illness & Substance Abuse

by
Nancy P. Masland, Ed.S

*To Sue,
Whose love radiates
to all ages!
Thank you,
Nancy*

Henri Nouwen, in his 'Daily Meditation' John 10:11: One of the greatest gifts we can give others is ourselves. Make our own lives, sorrows, joys, depair and hope available to others as sources of new life.

Dedication

This book is dedicated to Elizabeth Barnes Masland,
January 13, 1962 – June 26, 2014, beloved daughter and
sister, who suffered from both Chemical Dependency and
Chronic Mental Illness.

Your appreciation of nature and beauty
And above all, Your STORY of a "Living Death"
Overcoming all odds and finally
Finding freedom in GOD's love when
You let go and let God's will be done.
You fought the good fight
With all thy might
Your spiritual courage
Allowed you to risk all of
Your temporal life in order
To gain an Eternal one
You answered God's call
As a needed one
Your laughter, singing, dancing
Your piano playing, riding horses
Your incredible memory,
Love of family, of fun, freedom and style

"Ode To Betsy" by Nancy P. Masland July, 2014

Tell them in England if they ask
what brought us to these wars
on this plateau beneath the night's gray manifest of stars
it was not fraud nor foolishness
glory, revenge or pay
it was because our open eyes could see no other way.

"No Other Way" by Lou Kenton (1930)

Acknowledgements

This book dealing with a family's struggle with mental illness and substance abuse could not have happened without the encouragement and dedication of so many who supported the project through completion, for which I am most grateful and humbled.

I am especially indebted to the following:

Ellie Masland Wolcott, my eldest daughter, for her steadfast editing and writing. Rebecca Redelsheimer, for her help in co-leading the House of Heart, befriending Betsy and me, and drawing the cover design. My late husband, Bill Masland, for his commitment to improving the Arizona Mental Health System and for encouraging my writing. St. Francis in the Foothills Church, whose members became not only the House of Heart volunteer Board of Directors, but also some of our first residents. Their willingness to be interviewed and their candor in telling us their opinions will help others.

My educators through the years: Miss Catherine Doran Watson, English teacher at Miss Porter's School, Pat Troxell, English faculty at Bryn Mawr College, Dr. Aldine von Isser, Special education faculty member—Emotional Development—at the

University of Arizona, Barrie Ryan, English faculty, especially poetry, at the University of Arizona.

The case managers, nurses and doctors at La Frontera, and behavioral technicians and staff at Thornydale Ranch, as well as the many group home managers, who served Betsy and our family diligently and caringly.

My colleagues at IECA (Independent Educational Consultant Association), and NATSAP (National Association of Therapeutic Schools and Programs), for the thirty-year opportunity to evaluate therapeutic schools, colleges, hospitals, group homes, young adult recovery, and wilderness programs.

NAMISA and PLAN of AZ for their education, support, advocacy on behalf of the SMI.

The Gathering of Grandmothers, for their spiritual support and grounding for over 20 years.

And lastly, to those who helped under a deadline to edit, format, publish, and print the final copies:

Table of Contents

Introduction

House of Heart & Heartbreak has been brewing for many years, especially since my daughter's (Elizabeth Barnes Masland) death in June 2014. As a mother of a triple diagnosed - schizophrenia, bi-polar, and chronic substance abuser - who struggled for almost forty years with these diseases, I need to share my experience and hope. Many system improvements have occurred since 1976, and I want to enumerate the areas I engaged in during those years, so that families can sidestep some of the obstacles and thrive, as well as survive.

The Dual Diagnosis of Mental Illness combined with Substance Abuse is like other illnesses and yet not like them. This is not a parent's nor society's failure. This is a story of how families have dealt and can deal with Dual Diagnosis within the family. When we are caught up in the moment caring for a person with severe mental illness, our first response is to search for available help. The goal is not always sufficient to meet the needs of the family members surrounding the mentally ill individual. We must not only meet the needs of the ill person, but also of the family and the surrounding community.

This book is intended to be an aid to families addressing Dual Diagnosis in a family member. It will include a personal history, approach and methods in a real life scenario with the idea of providing our readers hope. Included will be ideas on how to keep the family safe, how to provide assistance while maintaining a healthy aspect within the greater family, and what we can do to provide the assistance to our family member in need. We will look at how we can maintain our own mental wellness. This book revolves around a group home established to provide care for multiple middle-aged women with severe Dual Diagnosis illness: the positives, the negatives and the challenges. A timeline detailing the progression of Betsy's illness and what part the HOH played in her treatment is included. This is the story of aggressive mental illness, the effect on families and the need to provide adequate housing for Dual Diagnosis Women.

The purpose of this book is to give direction to anyone, but especially those who want to better understand the dual diagnosis of substance abuse and mental illness and those considering beginning a group home for clients who suffer from Chronic Mental Illness, Chemical Dependency (including Alcoholism), or both (Dual Diagnosis). It addresses issues that parents, siblings, well-wishers, professionals, group home board members, caregivers, or clients have to face when running a group home.

This book includes interviews with the volunteers who formed a Board of Directors for this group home, as well as with the clients. Members of NAMI (National Alliance for the Mentally Ill, an organization that educates, advocates and supports families with seriously mentally ill family members) also contributed. This book also contains excerpts from Elizabeth Masland's journals with concurrent records made by medical professionals. My daughter's struggle with both Chronic Mental Illness and Chemical Dependency (including Alcoholism) and the inadequacy of treatment programs to help her motivated me to found this home and to write this book.

The intent is to share an experience with all the pros and the cons. In some things we succeeded, and in some we did not.

Dual Diagnosis in 1988

Double Trouble, Double Bind

In 1988, I submitted a paper to the National Alliance of the Mentally Ill (NAMI) Curriculum and Training Committee describing the double bind of those who suffer from both mental illness and chemical dependency. The purpose of this paper was to bring awareness of the conflicting philosophies of SAMHSA: Substance Abuse and Mental Health Services Administration and the Mental Health systems (NIMH), which results in frustration for everyone concerned. A person with the dual diagnosis of SMI (Serious Mental Illness) and SA (Substance Abuser) or Chemical Dependency (CD) fits into the category of *double trouble* for both systems and the family, and places both into a 'Double Bind.' Dual diagnosis is often misdiagnosed, by placing one or the other as the primary issue. State hospitals, surveys and studies report that 30-60% of SMI are CD, and 10-45% of CD are SMI. Management, treatment and placement of this client (family member) has been problematic, because of the different philosophies of both systems.

PART I: SYSTEMS CONFUSION

In 1988, these two systems had yet to fund programs for these clients appropriately, develop proper identification tools, treatment modalities, or placement facilities. In the 1970s, the mental health community had not recognized the dual diagnosis condition, and treatment options did not exist. In 2016, the dual diagnosis conundrum still exists, however, more research has been done to raise awareness of the issue. From that awareness, plans have been developed to treat this difficult condition. In this section, I describe "dual diagnosis" in detail to illustrate how complicated and difficult it is to diagnose and treat someone suffering from both mental illness and chemical dependency.

A. IDENTIFICATION/ DIAGNOSIS

Both diseases are brain diseases, which interfere with adaptive functioning, the ability to process novel and complex information, to filter distractions, and to plan, greatly affecting the patient's behavior.

Common tendencies in both the Chronically Mentally Ill and the Chemically Dependent:

- Onset between 12-25 years
- Chronicity (Repetitive and progressively serious episodes)
- Physical, behavioral in relationships and jobs deterioration

- Acute and psychotic episodes
- Self-medication: drugs or alcohol, which exacerbates the illness: (e.g. Schizophrenic clients often smoke marijuana; those with bipolar do coke, crack, and heroin)

This dilemma tends to confuse those diagnosing. Often, anxiety is lessened by alcohol or drugs, but then addiction creeps up. The progression of addiction is a separate biological process. A user of PCP or LSD can appear as an SMI, with a chemical imbalance. Often, CD hides an underlying psychosis, which can go undiagnosed. Prolonged periods of sobriety often reduce the psychotic symptoms, and the medications essential for cure can take effect.

TREATMENT

Currently, both systems in practice are in a 'double bind.' In 1988 an SMI client in a treatment center could not have medications as this would break the 'abstinence' rule. In a Mental Health Center (MHC), assaultive or other disruptive behaviors, due to chemical or alcohol withdrawal, are not countenanced. These were philosophies formed in the 1970's and have been changing, but substantive change requires funding and public awareness. Fear is a factor, as training does include both diseases, and rigidity prevails. The SMI client has a stigma of violence, irrationality, and poor social skills. One treatment center dismissed a request for medications by an SMI client, stating, 'Hell, we are all schizophrenic when we are drinking.' The truth is that now 18-40 year olds, labeled 'Chronics,' many of whom are veterans, are the homeless street people, ending up in jail or prison.

Many client's family members have given up on their ill family member. Many clients choose suicide, trying to exist in places that do not understand their needs. The dichotomy prevails. On the one hand, an SMI may respond and cooperate with a medically oriented, supportive, gently directive approach, and may resist an intense, emotional interaction; on the other hand, the CD needs intensity for intervention and confrontation to overcome denial and resistance, as well as a program, 12 step or SMART. With a support system, both the CD and SMI client can improve. For this individual, personal attachments decrease, and can lead to alienation, isolation and in some cases, an untimely death. Both systems must take responsibility for the dually diagnosed client. The 'double bind' remains, and they and their families are not served well.

PLACEMENT

The lack of progress in understanding the dually diagnosed client means there is large staff turnover.

Fear and ignorance dominate, rather than patience, awareness and acceptance among the staff. One of the legal issues in placing in a program is that an involuntary petition is possible only if the client is considered persistently and acutely disabled, gravely disabled, or a danger to herself or to others. (PAD, GD, DTS, DTO) With a voluntary petition, the client is willing to go into a restrictive setting or hospital, and can leave at any time he/she wants. Residents are a transient population which inhibit the benefits of the treatment programs. There is hope for the United States as other dual diagnosed programs are beginning in other states.

PART II. FAMILY PROBLEMS

Dr. Agnes Hatfield, PhD (NAMI Board Member and NAMI Chairman of Research) studied the DD population and found that the demands on the family exist even when the member does not live at home. Some of the questions that need to be answered are:
- What are the public or society's role and what is the family's?
- What are the rights of the family member and the family?
- Who knows the answers, the CD counselor or MH therapist?

- Why does the communication method the family member uses have to differ with both systems?
- What should family members do?
- Abstinence means not getting the right meds
- How does a family detach from their member?
- Will I be called co-dependent if I stay in the loop?
- How can the family maintain their sanity and integrity while being criticized by both systems?
- How much is the family supposed to participate in regarding legal, medical, financial, social, residential and recreational?
- Why are anxiety, guilt, and tension present?
- Who really understands my child and the situation?

When families were asked in Dr. Hatfield's study about their emotional state, they told her that they experienced constant anxiety, tension, wariness, depression, guilt, disappointment, frustration, and anger. They wanted the following, in order of concern, to be addressed:

- Relief from anxiety
- Training in techniques to motivate their family member
- Understanding appropriate expectation for their family member

- Aid during crisis and help when the family member is out of control
- Education about and help in accepting SMI-CD
- Help in decreasing friction in the family, between parents and with professionals, resulting from the family member's behaviors
- Help in alleviating guilt and blame
- Instruction on how to handle threats of violence
- How to make TIME FOR SELF

SOLUTIONS

In combining both systems to aid families as they cope, consider Dr. Alexander Hyde's *The Ten Commandments for Managing Schizophrenia.*
For the Mental Illness component:
- Get at least 8 hours sleep
- No stimulants of any kind
- No alcohol
- No marijuana or drugs
- Eat small amounts of white flour or sugar
- No junk foods
- Live in a supportive place surrounded by supportive people
- Love more than one person
- Do not isolate or live alone

- Exercise moderately each day
- Join the local Alliance for the Mentally Ill in each state and attend meetings which offer support, education and advocacy.

For the CD component:
- Follow a 12 step program (familiarize yourself with **SMART,** which includes going to meetings and getting a sponsor (both for AA, NA, Co-dependency and Al Anon).
  - Say the Serenity prayer on rising
  - Admit one is powerless over people, places, things
  - Admit one's life is unmanageable
  - One is willing to turn one's life and will over to the care of God or a Higher Power as you understand HIM/HER/THEM
  - Memorize the sayings : *First things first, easy does it, live & let live, let go & let God, Keep it Simple,*
- Focus on getting your family member into a recovery program that is concrete, practical, focused and consistent.
- Spiritual growth is critical, including reading, praying, and meditating daily
- Analyze your feelings and actions:

o Fears for and about the family
   member can consume those closest to
   the client.
o Family members want control but the
   family member's path is not in our
   control, and as rescuers, caretakers,
   and givers, we crave control and
   LOVE.
o Be detached not reactive.
o Suggest three ways to change
   behavior: conversion, decision,
   actions.
o Accept the fact that without
   something changing, someone
   precious will be lost.
o Do not enable or protect the family
   member from irresponsible behavior
   UNLESS the behavior is the result of
   her mental illness.
o First take care of oneself, be patient,
   and recognize and celebrate progress.

CONCLUSION

The dual diagnosis 'Double Bind' can be alleviated.
Most families are on the dysfunctional spectrum with
some being very dysfunctional. It is important to
recognize that society condones many addictive
characteristics such as workaholism, greed, playing

hard and working hard. When treating dual diagnosis clients, both the CMI and CD systems need to agree on philosophy, funding and appropriate service delivery. Both systems need appropriate treatment and placement facilities. In addition, families need to change radically and stop being reactors and enablers. Families must become honest, accepting and willing to adopt a dual recovery program to accept their dual diagnosis family member.

I implemented these practices in my relationship with Betsy. When we expressed affection to our daughter, we tended to help with problems, say 'I love you,' smile in a warm, friendly way, say how important she was to us. We would hug her and praise her accomplishments. We gave her caring and encouraging looks, telling her how special she was. We told her how much we cared about her, and we told her how much she meant to us. We gave her compliments, put an arm around her, and sat close. We acknowledged special occasions, such as her birthday, with a caring and encouraging way. We spoke in a warm, friendly voice.

When frustrated with her, I listened to her side of the story, discussed problems with her, tried to be fair, gave a frustrated look, calmly shared my feelings, left the scene or situation, and tried to patch things up.

Although stressed with work and Betsy's situations, I kept a close relationship with her. I was confident that she respected and accepted me. I put more time into my relationship with her than I put in my other work or activities. Doing my personal best is important to me. I was co-dependent in our relationship, and went into treatment for it in the early years. Sometimes, I was sad and frustrated, but not depressed.

When she wanted or needed a hug, I was glad to provide it. I tended to get over-involved in her problems. When she was upset, I provided support and comfort. I was very attentive to her verbal signals. I controlled myself, trying to be cooperative, especially about money. I could tell when she needed comforting, even if she did not ask for it. I tried to respect her ability to make her own decisions, but told her what I would do. I took care of my own needs before hers.

Elizabeth (Betsy)

On January 13, 1962, Elizabeth Barnes Masland (Betsy) was born in Philadelphia, PA, fourteen months after her older sister, Ellie, was born. Labor was induced. She was a healthy baby, weighing 8.5 pounds. For the first nine years of her life, Betsy, her sister, father, and I lived in the greater Philadelphia area. In those first nine years of her life, we moved four times, and Betsy and Ellie changed schools as many times. I worked as an educator in independent private schools, and Betsy's father, an MD from the University of Pennsylvania, worked as a researcher at the University of Pennsylvania. In August, 1971 we moved to Tucson, Arizona. I became the head of Green Fields School, a small independent private school, and Betsy's father began private practice as a neurologist. As the pressures of neurology, unresolved emotions from his youth and childhood grew, Betsy's father turned to alcohol. By the time Betsy was thirteen, her father's alcoholism was well-established, affecting the entire family.

Betsy was an amazing girl, talented in piano, horseback riding, and ice-skating. She was popular, beautiful and a leader. By eleven, Betsy started experimenting with different substances, starting with cigarettes and branching out into marijuana and alcohol. She started acting out in school. On April 3,

1976, on a field trip, Betsy brought a six-pack of beer which she shared with five other students. Betsy was expelled from Green Fields School. In 1977 she went to Miss Porter's School, a private boarding school on the East Coast, but was expelled in 1978. During the summer of 1978, Betsy experienced a psychotic break and began experiencing auditory hallucinations.

1978 was the year of the Camp David Summit when Jimmy Carter, Menachim Begin and Anwar Sadat hammered out what many hoped would be a permanent Middle East peace agreement. In 1978, 100,000 marched on Washington in favor of the Equal Rights Amendment, and we saw Muhammad Ali go fifteen rounds to beat Leon Spinks. In 1978 Harvey Milk, an openly gay man, was elected to public office in California, and AIDS had yet to become a national health crisis. 1978 would also distinguish itself as my most personally painful year, as both my brother and my mother died. That year my husband's alcoholism worsened. It was the year Betsy had her first psychotic break and hospitalization. She started on two medications, Stellazine and Lithium, and was admitted into Palo Verde Hospital in Tucson for six weeks. In spite of her illness and alcoholism which led to poor behavior, hostility, assault, and running away, Betsy graduated from high school in 1979.

1980

In 1980, her medications were changed to Elavil, which did not prevent Betsy from running away by bus to Tucumcari, NM, a nine hour trip from Tucson. Dr. Dennis Weston in Tucson recommended hospitalization, stating that Betsy needed treatment for longer periods of time. He said that she was psychotically depressed, but with intensive care, she could improve. In February, 1980 Betsy went to the Institute of Living in Connecticut and stayed there through December, 1981. The cost in 1981 dollars was $100,000 ($270,000 in today's dollars). During that time she regressed and socially withdrew. She escaped from the Institute to drink and swallowed detergent in a suicide attempt. During that time she took a combination of the following medications: Stellazine, Haldol, Prolixin, Impramine, Fluphenazine.

Betsy's Letters to Her Father during her Time at The Institute for Living

- July, 1980 - It's been really weird because I've made friends on the unit, but I still feel really lonely. I talked with the Dr, and she didn't understand why I still am depressed. Mom is coming which will be good. I can't wait to see her. It seems like a long time since the family has been together. Maybe soon, we will all four of us be together. My plans when I leave the hospital: I want to find an apartment and find a job or continue with my college career. I've discussed these plans with the Dr, and she thinks that I should live on my own, instead of at home. So I'll take her advice and live on my own or with another person, possibly sharing an apartment and splitting the rent. What do you think, Dad? Love, Betsy

- How's everything? I miss you a whole lot. I haven't been able to call home because of home restrictions. It's hard to get hold of anyone. It was so good to see you in May. Sorry I missed your birthday: HAPPY BIRTHDAY!

- Dad, I want you to know that I really appreciate your coming to visit me. It really means a lot to me. I know that we have had troubles in the past and that there will hopefully not be too many more in the future. I have learned to forgive and forget, but sometimes, it hasn't been that way. So what I'm asking for is forgiveness for all of the past experiences that have made trouble for both you and Mom. What I would like to do is start from here and work for a more meaningful future that includes my family relationships. I love you, Betsy

- 9/80 I thought I would drop a line to say "Hi" and also to see how you are! Things here are running pretty smoothly. I am also going out on a visit with my sister, and that should be kind of fun. Well take care and send my love to Mom, Betsy

- Though I barely see you, I think you're the most fantastic dad in the world!

- 4/81 - So how are things in good ole Tucson. Anything I might be interested in? I heard about the wedding from Mom. Tell me about the pets and weather? Is it time to go swimming? I signed out of the hospital last Sunday, but because of the reaction that I got from everyone (you, staff, Mom, my doctor) I am signing back in. I hope to move to a higher unit so that I can exercise some of the responsibilities that come with being on a higher one. Before I make any more plans I will talk with the Dr to see if she feels that I am ready to move up. Then, after 6 weeks, I will sign out to go to MV with Mom for the summer. How does that sound? A lot has been going on in my head about starting to get off my rear end and get involved in as many activities as I can. That way, time will pass quickly, and I will also be getting the therapy and help that I need. Well, enjoy life, & keep in touch, love you. Thanks for the beautiful Easter Lily that arrived. I am fine though I do miss you and the rest of the family very much.

- 10/1981: I know that my life seems to stop at a point of confusion, but I really feel that these next few months are going to be helpful to me in terms of understanding myself, where my feelings are coming from, and how to control my impulses. How do you feel about it? Do you understand that I am not always the easiest person in the world to understand or 'analyze'? I feel that although the institute can keep us too long, I sometimes feel that I might not yet have been here long enough. You know? I am really hoping that by Christmas I will be ready to once again, come out of the dark and out to or through the wall. If I am not making myself clear, please correct me. So, as the old saying goes. I miss you, Dad. Will I ever be well? I love you. PS. Caring is enough for me, as far as I'm concerned. Please call, as I feel that I am now ready to talk with you and share my feelings. Hopefully we will both come to some understanding, and we will be able to communicate our feelings (at least this is something that I am wishing for myself) because I know that in the past there has been, on my part, more than once, a breach of trust that I would like to learn from, because I now know that both you and Mom did your best to let us to learn from our mistakes by allowing us the freedom to make decisions that could have gone either way. I love you, Betsy

- November, 1981 - I love you and thank you for the check. I really enjoyed the card that it came in, too! How are things, the pets, weather ? I miss you so much. I can't wait until I am discharged and out of this place! I guess it means going through the system first, getting off AWOL, this unit! It won't be too long, though, I hope. I just finished writing in my journal before I decided to write you! I hope Mom has fun for 4 days in Mexico. I finished reading "A Christies' Curtain", and I might start Tom Robbins new book soon. I am working on a latch-hook pillow to finish; it's an awful lot of fun! How is the weather for bike riding? Any good rides recently? I had a good talk with the Dr, and I hope to talk with somebody soon. Enjoy yourself, Dad, and thank you again. I love you, Betsy

- July, 1981 - I'm feeling much better, although I was having kind of a difficult time last weekend. There seems to be a lot of ups and downs as the time passes. I'm working on a pillow to give Mom on her birthday, and I made her a belt which she has with her. I put on weight from all the liquids and am sweating in the heat. I hope to be taken off AWOL. I'm so sorry that I wasn't too talkative on the phone and have been kind of overwhelmed recently for the mere reason that a lot of big things have been happening, I am hoping that the Dr will take me off AWOL. My care plan person is comfortable with it, and I am anxious. I think a lot about the visit coming up with Mom. I hope our next talk will be easier for me to talk because I love you, Dad, and I know that I can't always break through the barriers of communication so that I am able to express myself. So remember that I love you, Dad.

- It has been good talking with you on the phone and getting cards in the mail. I really feel good about how things have been working out. Today was a good day for many reasons. I had a nice visit from mom after she met with the Dr. It seems that they had a good discussion. I did not have a session with the doctor, and I look forward to the next ones. So, how are you surviving the summer heat? I know that for me in Hartford, the heat is sometimes unbearable, so I can imagine what you are going through. It is good hearing about the family and about what has been happening with them; although I hope that you still have enough time for yourself. Mom brought me some Agatha Christie books that I am looking forward to reading, so you need not worry about my not using my time constructively. Take care, Dad, I love you, Betsy.

- June, 1981 - HAPPY FATHER'S DAY! Take care and I hope that it's a good one. Love you, Betsy

My Letter to Betsy Outlining Program Options to attend after The Institute

Dearest Bets,

I want to describe the options that you can consider in making your decision as to the next step, rather than have it all come verbally and at once at a meeting. I'm sending a copy of this to your sister, Dad, and therapist at the Institute. This is my latest understanding. More materials will be coming. Cost may negate some choices, but we will consider all that later. This list is in order of 'cheaper to expensive.'

Also, some depend on whether you are accepted, and are ready for the program; so, there are uncertainties. I have written Dad and asked him to come East 4/7-11/1982 over Easter weekend to help us with the decision and will understand if he cannot.

- AZ State Hospital- short term. On the Plus side: no cost, location, very structured, safe; On the Minus side: less individualized care; some acute cases and long-term , very sick patients

- Harbourview- a short term convalescent home located in West Haven (near New Haven) On

the Plus side: The cost is $40 a day; structured;
On the Minus side: mostly elderly

- Martha's Vineyard - Featherstone Farm- $40 a day; Ages 14-50 with prior hospitalization. Majority 25-35 yr old; 25 acres, abuts state forest and campground. On the Plus side: horseback riding, 2 hrs daily instruction $30 or in exchange for work, help building pottery shed; you would have 2 yr old foal named 'Just a Feather', rabbits, chickens, ducks, pigs, dogs, cats; pottery; you could have your own cottage @ $500 x mo; Food/board: $250 a mo. On the Minus side: too much independence too soon?

- Gould Farm, MA NW Berkshires: Interview, 24 hrs. On the Plus side: 40 guests —wide range of problems; good support system, Christian, beautiful setting, large acreage; progress to ¼ then ½ way houses. On the Minus side: $60 a day + $15= $75; need 20 hrs. work a wk. ; is it too unstructured?

- Wellspring, Bethlehem, CT —must be willing to work on self; interview. On the Plus side: individualized ; 5 residents live in a house on 5 acres, animals, garden, structured schedule; activities include: art, music, drama, poetry; On the Minus side: $125 x day.

After The Institute for Living

After the Institute, Betsy went to the Connecticut Mental Health Center located at Yale's Clinical Hospital where she continued to experience auditory hallucinations and act out angrily. From there she went to Gould Farm, in Massachusetts, which is the first residential therapeutic community in the nation dedicated to helping adults with mental health and related challenges move toward recovery. She stayed there until the end of 1982.

On August 1, 1982, my husband joined AA and began the long road to sobriety. I also gave up drinking alcohol.

By January 1983, Betsy had returned to Tucson and was living in the Kiva House, run by Intermountain, where she stayed until November when she was evicted as a result of abusing illegal substances. She was also in an unhealthy relationship with a man. After returning to Tucson, Betsy went on Arizona State health insurance (AHCCS). In the mid-80s she experienced ten hospitalizations. Between 1983 and 1990 she lived on her own with her common-law husband, as well as in a variety of group homes and half-way houses without him, such as Omega House and La Llave (a La Frontera facility). In April, 1985 I filed an Involuntary Petition (IP) for Domestic

Violence and DUI. Her SO was involved in financial fraud, dealing drugs, alcohol abuse, battering, and he was dual-diagnosed for substance abuse and Schizo-Affective disorder. Betsy worked at the Sheltered Workshop, a vocational rehabilitation facility, from November, 1985 through February, 1986.

Journal Entries Detailing an Eviction in 1988

The following are journal entries I made during Betsy and her SO's eviction from HUD housing in March, 1988:

3/23/1988 – Betsy said, "I am nauseous from the Lithium and will go to La Frontera."

3/24/1988 – I invited her to join me in Phoenix for the Walk for Conscience. I told Betsy that I would be gone attending the Walk at those times.

3/25/1988 – I phoned Betsy four times and did not reach her. I finally reached her, and she asked for $53 to pay for a broken window before they are evicted. A chair also had been broken. I refused, and I said her grandfather's $150 deposit should cover it.

3/26/1988 – Betsy phoned, and I suggested that she ask God's will and to look at the answer. I reminded her of all the drama when she is with her SO. I wasn't sure if she was listening to me. She asked me for money to get the vacuum and massager fixed that the dog had chewed. I invited her for lunch, helped her find the vacuum repair, and I agreed to handle the money issue on the first of the month. The vacuum repair was $10, and I agreed to take her for lunch to say goodbye to her grandfather who was leaving for the East Coast. I welcomed her to come back home if she agreed to leave her SO and the abusive relationship. I called to her room, and she told me that she had to be out of her room by noon. I told her that I could not change my plans as I had plans to meet two elderly relatives for lunch. I told her to call me at 2 pm. I asked her again to leave the abusive relationship with her SO, but she said, "I am staying with him." At 3 pm Betsy called collect from downtown, and said, "Mom, you were right. I should have left my SO when he broke my nose three months ago. I hate him. I won't be scared of him, his friends, his drugs, his cars. I don't know where he is, and my meds and everything are locked up. I can get a food basket in 40 minutes which will take care of food. I don't know why we were evicted. The only trouble is that I don't know where I can sleep. I have no money. My SO can stay in the apartment, but why not me?" I asked her what her options were. She said, "I can always go to Kino Hospital if they will take me." I said that I would call La Frontera and talk to the Crisis Worker to find a bed. She said that she didn't want to be in any of those schizo-alcoholic places. She could be at home. I called her sister who agreed to meet her at 4pm with a truck. I called Betsy back, and then I called Respite Care who called the Crisis Worker. The Crisis Worker agreed to a weekend bed, and she said she would meet us at 4:45pm only on the following conditions: Betsy's SO was not there; Betsy was sober; Betsy was voluntarily going for the weekend bed. He said he would talk to the coordinator.

3:45 – I tried calling Betsy's sister three times without success.

4:05 – I called the Motel and was told that the manager was up in the room with them. Betsy's SO answered the phone, and he said they needed $100 for the broken chair and window. He said that they needed a truck and that they had a house. Betsy got on the phone and asked when I was coming, and I told her that her sister was coming with the truck. I told her that I had arranged for her to meet with the Crisis Worker at Respite at 4:45pm. Betsy then hung up. At 4:15 the Crisis Worker called to say he was available on Sunday as well.

6pm – Betsy and her sister returned with the loaded truck. I again invited Betsy to spend the night at home if she would leave her SO. Betsy said, "NO." Betsy's SO drove up to help unload. He said that they would stay at a motel until they got a place. He said that they were staying at a friend's place. I gave them food.

7:30 pm – Betsy called to say that she was angry and that she didn't know what to do. Her SO got the $60 deposit (which was her money) from the motel. He is leaving to spend the night with his mother. She said that she was not wanted at home because of her father's and grandfather's attitude towards her. I said that I had given her alternatives. Betsy said that she knew. I told her to call the abused women shelters or Respite. Betsy's sister got on the phone and repeated the numbers, but Betsy would not give her address or number.

I felt that I did everything I could do and am looking at how powerless I am and feel. I keep praying. Betsy's sister said, "She is not taking her medications."

This is one example of our interactions during a crisis. After many similar crises, I finally wrote a letter to her which said "I am leaving for a business trip in one week and have tried to help you. I have offered and tried to get you help, both residential and medical. Here are the emergency numbers you can all. I am giving you two cartons of cigarettes and 59 cans of soda which should be enough to last you until I return. I have paid for your phone. I will not call or stop by because I need to 'let go and let God.' I will always love you. Mom"

On April 1, 1988, Betsy was arrested for Domestic Violence Assault, and required to spend one day in jail without option.

1990

In September, 1990 while Betsy was living on her own with her common-law husband, she was hospitalized after a weekend crisis and psychotic break. The rapid response MAC team did not respond because they said battery and abuse was the "only problem." Police had to remove Betsy from her residence. Betsy's case manager was declared incompetent, and we hired a private social worker to take Betsy to the hospital.

During the late 1980s and into the early 1990s, my husband and I set up Guardianships of Southern Arizona, an advocacy group whose role was to protect the client's Social Security Insurance and to be guardian, adviser, and advocate for the client. We also became involved in ADAPT, NAMI, and NAMISA. These were all young organizations, and resources for people like Betsy with a dual diagnosis were rare.

Guardianship responsibilities for Betsy included distributing finances to her. Money was a constant source of conflict between Betsy and me, and that conflict motivated me to rely on a third party guardianship organization to distribute Betsy's money. Initially, my husband and I were Betsy's guardians. GSA-Guardianships of Southern Arizona took over guardianship. Later, another organization, SCOPE, became the Representative Payee. In February, 2008 Project H.O.M.E. took over distributing Betsy's Social Security Income, which had ranged from $470 - $1000 a month with Food Stamps worth $17 – $30 month, over the years.

As her mother, I tried to help out with transportation for food and cigarettes, so they would be cheaper, but being involved with Betsy's needs and wants frustrated me. I did not give her cash because it was always spent on alcohol. I was concerned that Betsy's manipulation of money was unhealthy for all concerned. In the early 1990s, I worried about the lack of firm support from LFC working with PLAN to establish a new system for distributing money and for shopping. There was one instance when the SSA noticed they had overpaid Betsy by $1900 and refused to send her a check. I turned this over to GSA, her guardian for resolution.

In 1999, through PLAN of AZ, I set up a trust for $25,000 which was reduced because of her expenses to $10,000. A social worker would supply her with what she might need, such as food, Diet Coke, cigarettes, medication pick up, or doctor's appointments. PLAN's social worker would also check hygiene, take Betsy out for a meal a week, celebrate holidays, check in when she was sick, and provide transportation.

Since 1978, I continued to be involved in Betsy's care because every time I let the Mental Health or Alcohol government-run system, which are separate, take over, the ball was dropped and Betsy was left without appropriate care. Without my husband's and my efforts, very little happened for our daughter in the AZ mental health system. We tried to change the system. I was on the NAMI Board, and I helped start NAMI of Southern AZ , NAMISA. I have been Chairman of CPSA's SMI Advisory Board.

Despite our efforts to work with the system, there has been little follow through. As an example, after many days, I finally got a call back from Betsy's CM after saying, in the presence of my daughter, that she, the CM, could visit this Sunday, and we would have a 'staffing' this week with the MH counselor, the CM and her mother.' Nothing was scheduled, despite my daughter and I counting on both staffing and the Sunday visit. We were told there would be no staffing or visit because Betsy had not filled out the correct permission form. My frustration with the system was high.

In 1990, substance abuse treatment centers started refusing to take Betsy because of her mental condition, but in November, 1990, Eagle Crest Farm, a Mt. View Day Program, agreed to take her into their program, but after leaving the program, Betsy relapsed almost immediately. From June, 1991 to Fall, 1995 Betsy saw a different psychiatrist at La Frontera every two months. Betsy was told, "Betsy, you are too tough to handle." During this time Betsy was living in La Fiesta apartments which were supposed to be supervised, but her SO was able to visit and stay with her. At that time the ACCM (Academy of Certified Case Managers) supported the primary diagnosis of Alcoholism for Betsy, and the organization blamed my husband and me for failure to enter Betsy into treatment for her SMI. We sent a letter to Betsy's La Frontera case manager to increase interaction with Betsy who was non-compliant in taking her medications. In addition, she was not eating well, and she was taking Crack. During this time I had two major stress-related surgeries.

In March, 1993, Betsy gave birth to 5.5 lb. boy, who was healthy despite being low birth weight. I was there in the hospital with her during the emergency C-Section. Betsy had no pre-natal care, and no one was aware of her pregnancy. The doctors were split about saving the baby, but I advocated for both Betsy and her son. CPS intervened at the hospital, but on her son's fifth day, he went to live with Betsy's sister and her husband who had a seven month old baby. I wrote a letter to our extended family, and my husband's family responded to the letter and adopted Betsy's son when he was fourteen months old.

From March, 1993 to March, 1995, Betsy lived in the McDaniel's House, a group home where she improved her nutrition, but her alcohol abuse increased. After being hospitalized at Tucson Medical Center in April, 1995, Betsy started taking Risperidol. This new medication was a godsend. By the summer, 1995, Betsy was able to live in the Omega House, a structured 2200 square foot facility for forty clients, that was supportive and required attendance at AA meetings. As a result, Betsy was functioning better than she had since 1978. At that time the CPSA disbursed Betsy's SSI funds from the Department of Health Services.

By November, 1995, Betsy had moved to the Tucson House, a HUD, section 8, high-rise housing option that offered a stable setting and good security. Her case manager visited her on a weekly basis, and she met with the same psychiatrist for one year. After that brief year of stability, Betsy's addictions again drove her to change residencies frequently. She lived in twenty-four separate houses within a two year period during this time.

In 2007, I filed three Involuntary Petitions, and then in 2009 and 2010 I filed several Involuntary Petitions for Betsy to receive treatment.

My observation during this time is that the mental health system did not provide a secure, sane setting for detoxification of SMI clients. Betsy's anxiety increased during detoxification at the LARC treatment center. She self-medicated with alcohol to decrease anxiety. I also observed that case managers did not interact with families, nor were families offered support and assistance during the 1990s. Because Betsy's residence changed so often, her anxiety soared, as did the MAC team visits. I feel that at that time, protection and advocacy were a farce. Schizophrenia and its associated complications are known as 'a living death.' Will we continue to condemn an individual living with an SMI?

Over the years, Betsy experienced some non-mental health related medical issues. She suffered from Hyponatremia which is a lack of sodium. She had three abortions before she had a C-Section to give birth to her son. She did not suffer any long-term physical problems from any of her pregnancies or from the delivery and recovered fully. In April, 2009, Betsy was ticketed for failing to yield to a motor vehicle. She was intoxicated and living on the streets when she stepped out in front of a truck who could not avoid hitting her. The collision broke the upper part of her left arm which required surgery and took many months to heal completely. Betsy also suffered from ulcers, and her teeth and gums deteriorated as the alcohol, drugs, and illness took their toll. She suffered from side effects from the medications, such as, poor depth perception, dry mouth, dizziness, blurred vision, sleepiness, and rotten teeth. She eventually lost two of her bottom teeth. Betsy also had a negative result after having a biopsy of her breast.

The following sections include excerpts from Betsy's journals, records made by medical staff, and excerpts from my journals. Starting in 2007, I interspersed Betsy's journal entries with the medical staff records, as a comparison between what Betsy was experiencing and what staff was observing. Betsy's journal entries are indented and in *italics,* and the staff's records are in standard, un-italized text.

2000

>*Burning incense and thinking about taking my meds. It is still early. I want to get some cash —tee hee hee and buy SO a kegger at the liquor store with a buckle tap and a shit load of ICE! DES will not give me money benefits on my card because I am not eligible, and the SSI representative payee and legal*

guardian may lose my checks with direct deposit into the bank, so ,fuck that shit! I am broke and I need some cash so that when they open, me, myself, and I and Lover (I love him. True love, 4-ever!) can kick it at the house with some .. and watch the tv. They don't like me to drink because the asshole wrote me off. They think they are superior. I hate them, Fuck u asshole.

10/10 4am *— Significant Other(SO) is sleeping on the couch, and his friend is crashed out on the chair. Honey Bunny, my cat, is awake and so am I! SO came banging on my door at 1:30 am. I was asleep then, but I got up and answered the door. We went shopping with my money at the 7-11 to buy some stew, so SO can go on a quest with his friend. I have some food so he has something to eat. He will have to wait and find out if we have enough for a big one (sic. Keg??)or panhandle later for a better one !? I have $.89, so, I do not know if J wants to go with me or if I am going to have go by myself? Looking out the window, it is still very windy, 20mph, but it is starting to get light. Someone gave me 6 packages of Bandits, 100 packages of 2 cartons and 2 free ones. I had money from my SO that he spent with me on a bunch of ICE! So I told my SO that I would feed him* *since he spent all of that money. I receive money from SSI. I have all my receipts for PLAN of AZ and for CPES as they supervise me on their home care program here at Columbus Terrace Apts. I spent my laundry money on ICE, and it was really good. I am smoking Bandits, drinking a diet coke, and thinking of going to the store with my SO in a little while. I am listening to KLPX 96 Rock, and I still have my ROCK card. It is my favorite station. And have a nice day. 6am I left my SO home alone with the two cats, and I walked to the store and got some things. Then I walked home.*

We are short of lighters which I have lost. At 8am I walked back over to the store and bought milk and more Diet Coke , while my SO was still snoozing on the couch with CBS news on. Right now, Sally is on TV. I took my meds and then let the two cats outside on the balcony for a little bit of fresh air. They were playing with a twig – a branch from one of the trees. I brought it inside, and my SO awoke and asked what time it was. At 8:15 am the two cats are taking cat naps, and I am sitting at the table. My SO's friend is still on the couch. I need money for some ICE. I am dreaming about some ale, but I don't have money. I NEED A DRINK! My SO said he has some money at home, but he is still sleepy. I don't want to wake him. I am watching Channel 4 "Martha Stewart live." Mom called about the Grandmother's group at Wilma's ranch in Oracle at 7pm. SO is up and about. We're having a good evening together. I have the sun and the moon tonight behind the clouds, and the air is much cooler. I am watching Channel 13, and it is 60 degrees right now. The sun has not come up yet, and the stars in the sky are beautiful! It is a little nippy outside. I wore long sleeves. SO just had a bite to eat, and he says the mixture of alcohol and his meds makes him black out. I want one too.

10/12- *I awoke at 4am and walked to my SO's who said he was not going to his Dr.'s apt. at La Frontera Center. He has to go to City Court today. We took the Sun Tran and went together. I hope they drop the charges and throw it out of court. At 6:30am I walked back to my SO's who is still sleeping. I asked if I could get him some ICE. He said maybe later after he wakes up. He is still sleepy. The two cats are up and about. I am watching TV, reading the paper. I 'm here alone, wondering and waiting. At 1am it is raining outside. Yesterday, I got 6 packs of cigs, some money, and I took me shopping at Fry's. My*

SO cooked chili. We got in a fight, and he went home. I walked to the 7-11 and bought a 12 pk of ICE. I went and bought 2 Mickey's and gave one to my SO. He drank most of the ICE.
10/13 *4am – I woke up and watched Jerry Springer News. HB and I went outside for a breath of fresh air. Now I am listening to the radio.*

11 am - I saw J in his apt and brought him cigarettes. Then he came over, and I walked down 29th to get him a 24oz of Mickeys, ICE brewed ale at 5.8 alcohol. He left C to see HB and went home with A. Chef SO made a beautiful beef stew, and a more beautiful spaghetti dish for dinner! Chef SO goes to town.

10/14 *- I have kept an eye on the two cats. They are up. So am I, and I luv you. At 4am my SO just called me. I luv him! He is waking up.*

2001

1/24 5 am *- I have a diary now and am having fun writing every day. My cat is here. Ten mins until 7-11 starts selling. It is still cold and dark outside. My SO and his friend came over. KLPA is playing good rock 'n roll this am on the radio! I need some ICE but I don't have any money. I drink too much, my guts* *are killing me! My brain feels like it is swimming in shit & my back, hips, thighs, are aching. Like real bad. I am not in too good shape. My lungs are hashed from smoking & I have put on a lot of weight, will meet CM again for money. Same time- same place. Shopping day Fry's &Walgreens House check. Toodle-loo.*

2/4 *As I was writing in my diary, I have a powerlessness & unmanageability that does not stem from alcohol even though I do drink. But, from problems stemming from my family issues- my childhood-growing up in a different environment- not being accepted for who I am-Schizophrenia- (which I also think was misdiagnosed) & drugs & alcohol with a dysfunctional family environment which was very difficult & unhealthy for me to grow up in. Don't get me wrong, I love my life & when it is time for me to go- I will be ready even if it might be before my time! O well, I know God listens to my prayers to save my soul- spiritually & in His eyes to ask HIM for forgiveness. For LOVE, I have one that no one can take from me. True love 4-ever! No monies in the world could buy the love we have. My son knows! Our son is going to survive. I have faith he will make it home.*

2002

> *9/11 - Dear SO. Hello! It's me, Elizabeth. How are you? I miss you very, very much. I love you dearly, truly with all of my heart. I need to make amends to you for all of the bad choices and decisions that I have made in the past since we first met when we were children. My last drink of the Beast, ICE, 5.9% alcohol, was last Thursday morning. I went to NW Hospital ER, LARC Gateway Vida Libre, and right now I am at CDV. I am sitting in bed, writing to you, and I am still craving a drink!? The time is 10:10 at night. No more smoking tonight. Bummer! I am listening to KFMA, love line. I remember Goodnight sweet dreams. I luv u, HB & Casper, too! I hope you get to read this!*
>
> *Blast off! And the moral of the story is, HARE today GOON tomorrow! Goodnight, hugs and kisses oooxxx*
>
> *9/12 - 8 am got to go to group*

2007

A plan was set up to stay clean and sober: attend Alcoholics Anonymous meetings 3x/week, work with her sponsor, join 2 groups each week. Encourage and motivate Betsy: determination, patience, responsibility. Attend all scheduled appointments:

PCP, Case Manager (CM), Doctor, nurse. Betsy will take care of hygiene: shower, shave, clean clothes.

10/15 -To Bets: the prettiest lady in the world. I will always love you with respect, a beautiful lady forever. Smile always. Sunshine, you bring in the leprechaun's pot of gold.

November: Groups for Betsy to participate in: Chemical Dependency (CD), Small, Women's, 12 step, Spirituality. Betsy's intention are to learn more about and understand SMI, drug and alcohol addiction, face feelings of low self-esteem and problems with boundaries by participating in the self-esteem group, by meditating and with exercise.

2008
March - Compliant with COT and SMART for first 30 days, including one-on-one sessions, placement at CDV. Medication management by taking medications as prescribed.
May - Betsy is living in a stable living environment, in a group home, following COT. She is remaining compliant and is attending 5 groups per week which include Relapse Prevention, Stress Management, Addiction Recovery. Drinking is not allowed
June — Betsy went AWOL from SLS. She is having trouble coping and is stressed by her roommate. She likes Kino and the new Wrap Around Services. Betsy

likes mystery novels and meditation books. She said that she does not care if she dies, and she had nothing to live for. She cried when she talked about her son and COT. She was glad that her CM came to see her. On 6/18 she was discharged.

6/20 - With art supplies at SLS, she drew sun, rainbow, flower, grass with smiling face. She drew gold at the end of rainbow. Betsy spoke about family not wanting her to stay with them, and not coming to see her. She did not want to go to Mt. Lemmon, as she does not like riding in vehicles. Betsy never wants to go anywhere which inhibits the other residents because there isn't enough staff. Agape SLS. She does not care whether she lives or dies. There is no reason to live anymore. She felt that La Frontera cannot expect her to do sobriety which she cannot do. She copes with stress, cleans, smokes, showers and does chores. To relax she does deep breathing, lays down, and isolates. She related her family issues and that she was abused, and that they are dysfunctional. She lost custody of her son due to drug use when she was pregnant. The last time she drank alcohol was on 6/18. She writes her goals in her journal. She wants to live independently, not go AWOL, stop drinking alcohol, take meds regularly, follow staff directions, follow house rules, keep appointments, follow treatment plan. Her boyfriend and drinking caused her to lose her trailer. The coping skills she listed included: calling her CM, reading a book, writing in her journal, listening to the radio. I got her with earphones. She was concerned about weight and about eating too much. She wants to be sober but not in locked down.

6/30- She read the book her CM got for her. She hasn't been drinking and has been doing well.

7/8 – Betsy went AWOL on 7/4. She bought beer and came back wanting a "benzo" which is addictive, not helping cravings. She made use of WRAP (peer support). The trigger was the party atmosphere at the BBQ, and she felt horrible about it. Betsy needs to focus on tools to get through her cravings and triggers. She said it was stressful swimming with Mom, why? Learn triggers and deal with them better.

> *I am at the Ranch, and I am not feeling too well and am withdrawing from alcohol, caffeine, and tobacco. I am losing weight. The meds are not right. I LUV my family so much! I was having such a good time at home. The house to me right now means the world to me xxxooo. I relapsed- a major slip! It was like I was high just being there! Since the 1970's! WOW what a rush! I took all my psych meds and some of Mom's Ibuprofen. Then I walked down the road to Bear Canyon Circle K. I was not afraid-NO FEAR. I bought a bottle of light dry, Puerto Rican Rum and two tall cans of Steele Reserve 211 high gravity lager. I paid cash, chugged the bottle in 3*

drinks, and left the 2 cans by the road. It was good. By then, I was in 7th heaven, and I knew that I was going to get caught at the mailbox by Mom and my sister. I did not understand why my old state ID was in the mailbox.

Mom asked how much money and cash I had on me. She said: 'Get her'. Shit, I hurt! They got me in the car. Mom said I would be medically cleared at the hospital and taken back to the Ranch. I am now back at the Ranch. Man, what a trip!!!! I hate to say it, but, that ba-ba Rum was good! xxxooo I was having fun- a party. The family means much more to me. We have been talking on the phone. The withdrawals and cravings are extreme. Tomorrow there is an ART meeting, I have mixed feelings about being at the Ranch TR. We never get to do anything- no groups, therapy- none of that. Staff get mean. All they do is sit in the office, watch TV & eat. All the clients want to go to the store for Cigs, $, and caffeine. It seems like a lot of BS. But then again, it is good to be here! I don't know. Just have to wait to see what they say about it. The meds are messing me up. I am craving and having withdrawals. How sad!

7/9- It was suggested that Betsy go to PHF for 30 days rather than to an ECU bed which is not available at Kino Hospital. She is worse functioning, using poor judgment and risky behavior by walking around town intoxicated. She has little insight about her treatment.

7/14- Betsy went AWOL from Agape. The staff threatened to take residents to AZ State Hospital (ASH) or California. Betsy woke up in the ER. She took a cab to SLS where cops took her to Kino. She was upset about being cuffed by the police. Staff would not give her cigs which caused her to be upset. They were threatened with ASH if they didn't voluntarily go to Kino. Betsy is worried that her $ is at SLS and that other residents and staff do not like her. She has nightmares about one of the staff. She wanted another chance but was reminded that she ends up in Kino if left to her own devices. She does not seem to own up to her drinking. She gets upset when reminded of her drinking

> *Staff changes: 7-3; 3-11; 11-7 I hear them saying something about a cook-out at Mt. Rose, but I am not wanting to go. I just had a DC and Seneca, and I am still craving caffeine and don't feel too good. My head hurts. I think it is the meds. I am just hoping and praying that they don't do a dirty trick on me and try to throw me in the hospital. I hate that. If worse comes to worst, I would*

rather stay here at TR even though I hate it. I am secluded and isolated here. The horses are sad. They look like they're starving and sick. Somebody abused them. I feel bad watching the animals suffering. It is that bad. I love horses and animals. Humanities-Serenity- I feel for the people, too. Sanctuary, Safe place. No HARM CONTRACT. I feel violated by staff and their clients. Most of them don't even have a high school degree, diploma, or any college or university education. I just don't want to be used, abused or misused any more. They probably don't understand a word I say. Do you know what?! I really don't dare. I am dying to get this all on paper, trying to – so I don't explode. If they turn on me or throw me in the hospital I will resent them. I want to talk to Naomi or Ron about a step-down program. This is Level II- I need my freedom, and this place is out in the middle of nowhere. I am sad. Forgive me, God. They better not put me in lockdown. No cigs, no caffeine. With discharge papers from TMC. I am struggling through today. Right here, right now. Living in the moment. ONE DAY AT A TIME.

We are in the van going to Circle K, and I hope we don't get in a car accident. It is pretty scary! They want some cook-out. I am upset, and they would not let me have my DC! I am at a park down by the river with everybody. It is nice here. I want to go AWOL and go get something, but I can't. They won't let me. From right here, I don't want to go back to TR. A big K cola, and I'm going to drink it. I am still at the cook-out with Hot dog buns and beans. I want to run away. We are still at the park. I tried to call Mom. It is starting to get dark. I am hoping tomorrow I can go to step-down, someplace closer to Tucson. I don't think I can make it at TR much longer. I don't feel that it is anymore therapeutic in my recovery. I want to go on more outings, groups, meetings, someplace where I feel safe. No more threats, intimidations, harassment. I'm homesick. They don't like me at MR (MT. Rose). I need to be someplace with more positive energy. I am afraid. It is getting dark and we're still here. I just feel confused trying to get back on track, stabilizing, maintaining since my last relapse. We left about sunset. It was dark driving, but we stopped at Circle K and bought 2 1-liter bottles of DC. I was asked to give them to staff, and I refused. She is going to document it. I wish they would leave it alone. I feel sick again. It's not like I'm doing drugs or alcohol in here. I'm not.

Withdrawals: I need my caffeine, cigs, meds, and bed. I'm scared of staff. I wish they would be nice to me. Well anyhow, I made it through the day. I LUV U home. Family bless you and goodnight! Until tomorrow, I pray it will be a good decision for all of us ! Goodnight!!!

7/18- She is upset being in PHF and fears losing her Mom and Dad being in there, locked down. When she drinks, she realizes she hurts herself and ends up there. She wants to be at CDV or TR . A suggestion was made that when she wants to drink that she think about what she wants. Drinking keeps her from getting these things. Believe in herself; no matter what she feels others may feel about her.

I really wanted those passes. I am hoping I can see and visit with family again. I LLLLUV them! I miss home very much; I'm homesick. Mom and Dad are getting old. I don't want to lose them. I hope they outlive me because I don't know where I would be without them! I am very sad. I took my meds, but it doesn't help. I gave money for diet coke. Then they start manipulating and stipulating me, telling me that I can't have any. It is making me sick, literally physically ill! I feel like I get ripped off. Trust issues. They think I am untrustworthy- now let's see if they are. I hate myself. There is so much negative energy; it is not good for my recovery. I have been here since last summer. I think it's time for me to head on down the road or at least to a step-down program with more privileges, less restrictions, more independence, more freedom to grow into recovery. I am on restriction which sucks. I hate this place so much. I can't stand them. I am talking to ART about getting me out of here. This is not therapeutic for my recovery. I need out of here! I am scared! I don't trust the people here. I am sorry about what I did-so sad, but true! They're playing Lynyrd Skynyrd on the radio. I am waiting for my diet coke to come back. My head feels sick. I do truly love my phone calls home (family, especially DAD, pets) Hi Ho! I dream as a wish to be there. I LUV HOME. It is hard for me here at the RANCH. I hope they come back soon from the store. I need my caffeine fix. I want my change and a receipt. I have not eaten all day. I am going to be skinny again-then ATTITUDE OF GRATITUDE, POSITIVE THINKING, SERENITY PRAYER. I am not a bad person trying to get good; I am a sick person trying to get well. I listened to Mom and have been journaling and reading. I am sorry about my diseases, but it was a good

BOTTLE! I wish I had had time at home to drink it all! Oh well, back to square zero!

7/22 Passive aggressive approach to getting her needs met. She waits to be asked what she wants. She is soft spoken, sheepish, sad and worried. She is now in the Milagro unit at CDV, and likes it better than PHF. Two mellow roommates. Writing in her journal helps her with her emotions. She can smoke any time she wants. She is calmer and less agitated. She smiled and seemed happy.

7/23 Betsy is sleeping a lot. She is more assertive and directly addresses her needs with staff. She has better eye contact and is smiling. She needs to take meds as prescribed and attend appointments. She needs to participate in activities, in service and discharge (D/C) planning. She asks about D/C over and over again. She went on outing, showered, and took meds without cues.

7/27 – She was in a pleasant mood but is indecisive about the next step.

7/28 – She read the book 'Anger' and it helped her out. Her last drink was on 7/8. She wants Risperidol, as other meds give her blurred vision, muscle tension, nausea, dizziness. She is worried about making new friends and was told not to worry as she was a likeable person. She worried about her Mom and Dad getting old. She said that she wished they could live forever.

She thanked staff for the time and for giving her a radio, books, and journal for her sobriety.

8/5- She is delusional, seeing snakes. She is angry and would not engage.

8/18 TR: Moving to TR was hard time at first, but Betsy is now more engaged in treatment. Her paranoia, anxiety and delusions were decreasing. She had been clean and sober for 33 days, and she wants to stay at TR. She is improving, attending groups, communicating with staff, doing chores. She wants to remain at TR, as it's a new opportunity and 'way of life'. She understood that drinking was why she was at TR. She writes in her Journal, and she is aware that she will struggle with alcoholism and SMI all her life. She read her journal out loud that she was angry at revocation. Her husband annulled their first marriage and left with another woman. Her family does not accept her for who she is. The medical staff suggests that it is more important that she accept who she is and be happy with herself. She said that kids in school used to beat her up, that her father broke her jaw, and that he had her committed. She said her sister beat her up. She also said that her father used to drink and drive with her in the car. Females are degraded in this country. She tried to enlist in the military, but because of SMI, could not. The world is messed up. Suggestion: don't worry about the world because she can't fix it. She can only help herself. She did 'time' for a crime she did not commit. She is still in love with ex, and she is upset about her Mom taking her money. She believes death looks better than institutionalization. I encouraged her to stay sober. At TR she was sober. She is still journaling, and her therapist gave her another notebook. She seemed upset in general.

She seemed worse and did not want to talk with family. She talked to herself and seemed very defensive.

9/3- Betsy likes books CM checked out for her, and she said that she had a lot out of them. She went on a day pass with Mom. Betsy is worried about Mom's health problems. Mom assures her that she takes good care of herself. Good groups for Betsy. She stays out of arguments with other residents. She is worried about Mom. She has been 50 days sober. Mom is concerned that at Circle K she stared at the liquor section, and she is concerned about Betsy's need for dental help. When she goes away for her work, Betsy feels 'abandoned'. Betsy is functioning well, and she got a pass for lunch with Mom.

9/8- Betsy is upset because she missed her scheduled dentist apt. She woke up very upset and could not leave TR. She is doing better now.

> *9/10 – I want my things back. I miss home. I lost everything. It hurts. I need to go to Tucson soon! I am practically ready to get my own place. But, I am so scared and afraid that that they will lock me up – dirty trick – and*

abuse me some more. I have been going
without since last summer. They have not
treated me too nice here. The Agency, La
Frontera. Sometimes, most of the time I feel
sad, hurt and scared! My psychiatrist has
been prescribing me the wrong medications.
My PCP wants to perform OB/GYN on me.
My dentist practically killed me, and now
they want to torture my breasts.

9/11- Revoked: Betsy ran away from La Frontera and could not be found. History of substance abuse and of running off to be found passed out in public place by cops.

9/12- Checked into TMC but left without discharge.

9/17- Betsy is withdrawn, quiet, depressed using a low tone of voice and sullen demeanor. She is usually talkative and polite.

9/19- Betsy went AWOL from La Frontera Center with a boyfriend and had a few drinks. She had had 60 days of sobriety. Betsy feels bad about the relapse. Do not give up. Cops took her to Kino, then to TR. She got hurt, but she can't remember how. She was well groomed, eating, drinking. She felt bad about relapsing. She was uneasy, anxious, and pacing with a worried expression mixed with smiles.

9/23 – Betsy attended an ART meeting and local AA meetings. She met with her CM for support. She is having a problem staying focused. Scotty Fisher (nephew) died. He had been a big support. She was a bit sad but quickly switched to caffeine issue. She feels worse from less caffeine. It is hard to wake up without her coffee. She is going to St. Francis for the memorial service. Her chores are Ok, but she is anxious with a worried expression. She is fidgeting. She said, 'I have a lot to deal with: new doctor, nephew dying, a lot of changes.' She expressed sadness, anger, confusion and was tearful with her head in her hands. I may not have understood what happened. Agape was the best SLS as others are too unstructured or too loud. Mom is worried about telling her about Kelly, her best friend with a malignant tumor who is in hospital. She agreed to tell her back at TR with support system. Betsy complained that she did not have enough independence and that staff did not treat her nicely. She gets angry and takes it out on her roommate. She hides $ and denies it when caught. She said she was letting things out while dealing with her nephew's death.

> *This is it! ART meeting. I feel like shit. Wake up and feel the pain! God, why didn't you take me last night? I am just going to wait and see what they say; hopefully, it will be a good decision for me!? Maybe!? I hope so!! Right now, I took my meds, made the bed, had a Diet Coke, Caffeine, Seneca. I stink and need a shower!! Just tried Mom and got a recording. I want to go home so bad; to be*

there for them. It hurts! I don't want to lose my family! Right now, they mean the world for me. Luv U XXXOOO – I want to go home. Staff are mean, and they won't let me. A lot of negative energy in this place. I read "The Daily Word" – good. I'll try to make it through another day – today. I hope time passes quickly! Good group.

Next day: Good morning! Good night's sleep. Had a cigarette, a Diet Coke, made the bed, read the "Daily Word" and weighed in at 129 lbs. I can't wait to go to my PCP. I hope to hear from Mom.

From a letter she wrote to me: I think they killed him [Scotty]. I miss and kiss you. Thank you for everything that you have done for me, your daughter! God Bless You. You are the best Mom in the world! XXOO Luv & Hugs From me to Betsy: Keep up the good work. You are worth it! I love you so much and support you. Serenity Prayer helps.

9/30 – She did not want to leave TR. She did not feel safe and felt she would end up at the hospital or on the streets. She needs help and seems to know what she wants for her recovery. She had passes both for church and for lunch with Mom, as long as has rides and doesn't have to take the bus. She is doing chores, participating in groups, and her mood is up having gone to church.

I am mourning Scottie's (Scotty Eric Fisher), Dad's cat, my friends, my son: suicide; grieving. I am hurt! I miss you, XXXOOO John Grible Myers (6/26/1962), born in Akron, OH, moved to Iowa, then California, then Arizona. He lived in the Marshall Home for Men, Anny too! True luv forever. Yours, EBM, "B", "Bet", Betsy, Elizabeth, Bii-Bii, Bye-Bye

10/7- Betsy has had a lifelong dependence on alcohol. There was an ART meeting. Betsy agreed to discharge. In November she would go to SLS, start attending AA meetings twice a week. She had a worried expression, but smiled back.

They came back with everybody and with a 12-pack of 12-oz cans of Diet Coke, and they brought me back the receipt along with a lucky penny. Yum, I am going to enjoy it. I will start keeping track of that and of cigarettes too. Remember what they say: Actions speak louder than words. I am going to shut up and start listening more. Look and listen. I am completely looking forward to the ART meeting. Let them lay it on the line. I hope I can stay or go to someplace less restrictive. I hope they won't be mean to me. Maybe after I can get this heavy load off of me, to start fresh, brand new with a good, positive, healthy way of life! I hope my

*family still loves me, understands and accepts
me for who I am because I will always luv
them unconditionally forever-4-EVERY!
Forgiveness. I need all the support I can get.
God has the final work in my world – final
judgment. Turn it over – Let go; let God.*

10/24 - She liked the AA meeting, and she read some
of the philosophy books that her Mom got her which
helped her with her emotions. She is motivated to stay.

10/28 - She wants more responsibility and less
restrictions. She wants to attend 2 AA meetings and
have off site passes. She participated in the
conversation, voicing preferences and complaints.
She is tearful that she was only going to be at TR for
1 more month.

*Yuck, I am about to lose my teeth! I can't wait
to get out of here. Where am I going after
discharge from Thornydale Ranch? Like my
grandfather, Gamps, used to say, "Neither
borrower nor beggar, nor lender be. Stay
healthy, wealthy and wise. Eat, Drink and
Be Merry."*

10/29 - She likes Prolixin to help her keep her mood
stable. She said she feels stable. She is well groomed,
bright and social.

11/3 - She has her 30 day AA chip and is smiling
engaged in light conversation.

*I am content when I am happy and my needs
and wants are met. My hopes and dreams for*

the future are to be outpatient and discharged from the hospital. I like myself most when I am doing good, am being productive part of life and following rules. I like myself least when I am in trouble and my warning signals start coming up. I feel disappointed when I have to be in the hospital. People think I am a kind, understanding, likeable, outgoing person who has a lot of friends. I value being alive most and am enjoying life – happy, joyous and free. One negative trait I have is that sometimes I make mistakes. I am only human and not perfect. One of my positive traits is that I am outgoing and willing to help others recover.

The side effects of my medications are weakness, blurred vision, dry mouth, and toxicity. The stages of grief are denial and shock, anger, bargaining, depression, and acceptance. Will you be my Valentine? XXXOOO Guess who? The light is bright; the sun is fun; the sky is blue; the grass is green; and I love you! Music is light. Light is color; color is sound; sound is pictures; pictures are words; words are songs; songs are love; love is you.

11/5 – The goal is to discharge from Thornydale Ranch and address substance abuse issues. She has been at Thornydale Ranch 4 times, and though her functioning is improving, she may be ready for a lower level of care.

11/7 – A Cost benefit analysis was done for Betsy by the SMART program. She connects socializing and drinking, but she knows that it gets her into trouble. It is bad for her health and thinking. She put a lot of effort into her plan, goals, and wants to get closer to her family again. She is thinking about the SLS Edison House for sobriety. At the ART meeting, she said, ' I will just sit there and listen to what you people have to say about me.' She was going to try to keep a positive attitude about the ART meeting by doing breathing and meditation. She seemed suspicious about the meeting and about what would happen. She is anxious and walking in circles as if going AWOL.

11/8 - The meeting went well but she seemed anxious.

11/10 - The nurse reported that she is pleasant, social, talkative, disorganized, tangential

11/13 – She said that she would recommend Thornydale Ranch to anyone 'because it was so good to me'. She discussed going to see a doctor about her breast lump. At first she was hesitant but agreed after discussing responsibility. She is maintaining a healthy weight.

11/13 – She got a pass for lunch with Mom

11/19 – She is very anxious about the upcoming biopsy

11/20 - Staff removed caffeine restriction as incentive to go to oncologist appt.

11/21 - She discussed how drinking makes her feel. She is depressed the day after. I had trouble dealing with emotions. They would overwhelm me, and I would isolate. It is better to catch it early, and I recognize that it is important to take care of ourselves. She seems to have more insight into her drinking by connecting depression and drinking. She got a pass for church and lunch with Mom. She feels better and is going for biopsy which shows a sense of responsibility.

11/24 - She was better and had nice time at church. It was uplifting to see her mother.

11/26 — She has a new violent roommate which makes her anxious. She is clenching her fists with a worried expression.

12/1 — She is extremely anxious about the move, but CPES said they still needed an interview before the move.

12/3 — She is in good spirits and is looking forward to a step down. She is well groomed, bright and social.

12/8 — She is feeling good and likes Thornydale Ranch. The biopsy came back negative. Prolixin has side effects: blurry vision, dry mouth, Akathisia; Risperidol did not have side effects. She has a pass for 12/20/21. She is cooperative and happy. She will take a Valium before the dental appointment on 12/

11. CPES runs a four bedroom house with 24 hour care. Level III. Betsy is experiencing body dysmorphic thoughts.

12/15 – She receives Passes when behavior is consistent and appropriate.

12/16 - She was out with Mom for the day.

12/17 - She has been sober for 90 days. She is feeling good and has agreed to AA meetings. She feels healthier and is thinking clearer. She feels blessed for having the chance to be at Thornydale Ranch and to get her life together. She is excited about moving to her own apartment. She has improved, and she appreciates her sobriety. Despite taking 5 mg Valium, she could not go to the dentist because she was too anxious. Betsy was happy when she was told that she does not have Tardive dyskinesia and akathesia. She wants a Judicial Review (JR) to have her COT(Court Order Treatment) dropped. She needs four teeth removed, but she refused even though not doing it is a health risk. She said that she the right to her own lawyer. She is agitated and confrontational.

12/26 – She said that to deal with the drink temptations, she would call someone, write it down, and read. She can think about the past consequences of her drinking and that will help her say no. She feels Empowered to say no and to feel good about herself. She has been sober for 100 days. Her medications are helping with cravings, and she is open to AA meetings. She is waiting for CPES licensing. She is polite and cordial.

12/29 – She is sleeping and eating regularly.

12/30 – She got a pass to be with MOM. She said, 'it's going great'. She was friendly and happy.

12/31 – At the Nurse appointment she was smiling, positive, and she thanked her Case Manager for working with her. She is content with where she is living, and she feels Thornydale Ranch has helped her become healthier. She said, 'I feel so healthy right now.' She is able to go out and smoke alone without a check that she doesn't run off.

2009

1/9 – She is grateful for being sober and for having the chance to get her life together and for attending AA meetings to build support. She is optimistic and confident about sobriety and AA. She wants to stay with Mom for her birthday. She is cheerful!

1/15 – At La Frontera Betsy was smiling from ear to ear. She had a great birthday (1/13/1962) on an overnight pass with Mom. They watched a movie, ate steak, went out to dinner, and attended an AA meeting. She was friendly, spoke in detail about the visit, and she wants to spend more time with family because she feels that it is the most important to her. She was laughing. She has been sober for over 100 days. When asked about the temptations in town, she said that she knows what to do now: journal, call someone and talk about it. She knows the consequences if she drinks: revocation, hospital, hurting herself, and not remembering. She knew clearly how she got to Thornydale Ranch.

I weigh 136 lbs. I had an offsite overnight pass from Thornydale Ranch to go home. For me, I enjoyed being there, but the problem is that I stayed up all night. Uh-oh! Oh-no! I kept everyone up all night. I feel bad. I am sorry for keeping them awake all night. How awful! Mom drove me back. We had Taste of Texas! It was good! Delicious! There are some leftovers in the Thornydale Ranch icebox. We also got Starbucks coffee, Diet Coke, and ice. I am going to start keeping track of my things, per Mom's suggestion. I think that it is a really good idea! I love to journal! Thanks, Mom! It has been some time. I look forward to this week when we meet again. I need to cash my check and want to go to sleep. After staying up all night, I am tired and need my sleep. I pray for everybody at home to have a good night's sleep peacefully after my keeping them awake all night. I hope they are not mad at me. I really feel bad about that, and I am sorry. Forgive me. I love you all. Good night's sleep for them and for me too. Good night! Beautiful sunset! Sweet dreams. I have three trays of Valentine's cookies from

Walmart that I want to give to Mom. I do not know how many cigarettes or sodas I have, as they are locked up.

LETTER OF APOLOGY HOME
I feel terrible about my behavior last night. I owe you an apology. I am truly sorry about what happened. I would like to make amends and to say to you that it will not happen again. I hope that you can find a place in your heart to forgive me for what I did and to understand I am not perfect. I make mistakes and for that I am sorry. I will learn from my mistakes and move on. Mom and I are talking right now. Forgive me??!!??
Love you always,
Betsy

(Back to journaling)
I want to come clean about what happened when I was home for the overnight. At Walgreen's I bought Lubriderm but also two shooters of Captain Morgan Spiced Run and walked back to lunch. I saw my pony, Apache Red Eagle, a 14.2 hands, roan, registered appaloosa quarter horse [Apache Red Eagle has been dead for 30 years. Maybe Betsy was

having hallucinations.] . Then at CVS, I bought Benadryl and two more shooters of Bacardi Light Rum. Whew – one great day!! When we got home, I took the whole box of Benadryl, the four shooters, a lot of Buffered Aspirin, Metalife, Ibuprofen, along with my regular psych medications. AND IT WAS GOOD! I had two showers and all I could eat with a lot of caffeine. I was with my favorite people, pets, pool, vegetation, Friendly Family Palm Tree, and the St. Francis statue. My love to you, Masland Family, the greatest in the whole world! I love you, me, myself and I. Yummy, yum, yum. It was at the end of the day, and we had an extra delicious dinner. I saw two movies. Lily, Lilith, Lilea is Bev's dog, but she is having heart surgery, so we have her. I could not sleep even though I tried. I wanted to, but I really wanted to party rockin' all night to the morning light, and I did. I also drank a lot of soda and Starbucks. On the way back to Thornydale Ranch we had a blue Texas Burger. I still love my drinks, smokes, good food, a lot of heavy medicine, and good people. There's no place like home. I miss you! I started journaling again. The rum was really good. I needed it! A fix.

After returning to Thornydale Ranch, I listened to the radio, 107.5 KMYT, and I called Mom. The dogs were fighting which scared me. Say, "Break it up!" or "Call for help!" Protect them Lord. No more fighting. It scares me. I just got yelled at about too much caffeine. I don't need to be yelled at. They are mean and haven't shut up since they got here. The house is too noisy and too loud. It bothers and disturbs me. Somebody is always going off: yelling, shouting or fighting. They scare me. I am afraid of them. I won't talk to anyone here; they get mad at me for no reason. This is torture. It's a pig pen; the slovenly slobs. It hurts being here. I feel sorry for the animals. It is really un-alright, not OK. I have put on extra weight like unwanted luggage, a bunch of garbage. I don't need it. It is a long walk to get to the bathroom. It hurts because I go frequently. We are the only ones without a bathroom.

1/21 - One staff member is mean to her and hassles her when she uses the bathroom at night and smokes outside. She has been sober 131 days, and she does not want to be out on the streets again.

1/26- She had a pleasant visit with Mom, but she drank too much caffeine and did not sleep well.

I weigh 130 lbs. It's another beautiful morning. The sun is shining; the birds are chirping; the skies are blue. The horses have been fed. My roommate woke me up chewing Tootsie rolls, but I fell back asleep. I hope Mom and everyone got a good night's sleep too!

Rebecca visited me, and we saw the horses, Poncho, and the pot-bellied pigs. Staff make us beg for what's ours. Extortion, exploitation, molestation to the clients. They are mean: no therapy, no groups, no meetings, no transportation, nothing. It's the worst: mental illness and substance abuse in Southern Arizona. They have no schooling for treating severe mental illness, substance abuse, and family problems. They treat us like garbage. They are abusive. I hate staff. The staff-client war is Fucked-Up. I have caffeine restriction: 8 drinks a day. Staff says they are going to do something like go to the store and then they usually don't. We have to ask them. I have an option to move to CDV or New Directions. I would like to rent an apartment: a studio or an efficiency. It would be nice. I'm calling home. Staff took clients to the store. Thank goodness they are gone. Now I have a bit of quiet time.

2/10 – Betsy will be discharged to New Directions on 2/18.

> *I weigh 139 lbs. I read about joy in the "Daily Word." I am feeling pretty good this morning, a little better. It is the weekend, and I'm going to enjoy it. I hope they don't get angry with me – grumpy, grumples. I am listening to the radio with the light on, happy, joyous and free, sharing our experience, strength, hope, and courage to carry on, ONE DAY AT A TIME. Yeah!! I will call home to say, "I love you all out there." Hi!Ho! I am going to have a great day, no negative behavior: just smiles and a lot of love. I saw the moon outside – beautiful. I love you, Tucson! Project Home, an organization that helps others manage effectively, sent my check. I need my alcohol and drugs. I am sick, yes. They have nothing for me here. Use, abuse, misuse me. I need revenge; I am hurt; I need out of here, or I might die. I cashed my check at Walgreens, and I bought 1 shot of Bacardi, 1 box of Benadryl, new shades, Diet Coke, and green tea. Thank God for a GOOD DAY! Tweek!*
> *The animals are hungry, and the staff are making a big mess of Superclean Saturday. These people are crazy, insane, very abusive, mean. It's disgusting how perverted they are.*

I am upset. Staff drank my Starbucks. I had to pay cash $ for them. I can't open the window to let the sunshine in, so the room is dark. I hope I am not sick, but I have a sore throat and a headache. Somebody took a lot of cash from my purse. Thief!! I have no more coffee/soda. I know I didn't drink all of them. Bummer, I think staff drank them.

2/11- Betsy cut back on soda and cigarettes. She is excited about moving to town and off Court Ordered Treatment.

I am happy because I am leaving on 2/18. I have been here since July, almost 8 months. First Kino, then PHF, Next Casa Milagro, and finally Thornydale Ranch. Court Ordered Treatment has given me new opportunities and time to think about things. I have been able to really get my life in order. I have changed a lot since July. Thornydale Ranch taught a lesson that I will never forget. I am ready to transition to New Directions. I feel complete with my stay at Thornydale. I will be moving on the way to something good! I hope! I am willing to give it my all and to go to any lengths because I want it. I will miss it here – the horse, the people and the place. But something new is happening for me. I am going to be good and do my best. Hopefully, my Court Ordered Treatment will be dropped, and I will follow up with voluntary mental health treatment at La Frontera. I hope so. I am really thinking 'Home,' and I am excited about the move. Yeah!

2/13 – Betsy visited ND, and she knows that can't leave for 30 days. She has accepted this. Betsy was happy to take care of the horses.

I hope New Directions is a better program and that I can get well and feel better. It is closer to home. I want to do my best. I can't wait, but I must say that I will miss the animals, especially Victor, the bay Wakin, and Poncho the goat! I am sorry I woke up early, but I am in pain. My sleep is bothered and disturbed. I don't feel too good. I used to sleep just fine, wake up refreshed, and be ready for a new day with energy. But, not anymore. Maybe it will get better when I leave. Nobody ever bothered me when I slept alone. Now being around other people disturbs me. They are constantly asking me for my money, soda, coffee, snacks, cigarettes, and talking shit about me. I could have saved more money but it has all been frittered away; kiddies getting their goodies from the candy store. I hate it! I could have saved my $! I pay $400 for Room and Board at Thornydale Ranch, so I'll get money back when I leave. Well I am going to have a good *day, read 'The Daily Word:'* <u>*Silent Unity on*</u> <u>*comfort*</u>*. It is good. I am going to call Mom.*

2/18 – Betsy needs to admit, or she will lose her bed at New Directions. She is excited and in good spirits. She seemed overwhelmed and shy with the transition to the IP rehab program.

2/20 - Betsy is having a hard time sleeping. She likes her roommate, and she is participating in groups and activities.

2/23 – Betsy went AWOL. She was hospitalized, and she was nervous, unsure, and perspiring. It is intense to lose someone from the program. Betsy had a relapse. She fell down, and she had to go to St Joseph ER for detox and then back to New Directions. She is worse, and she fell and hurt herself. Betsy is having a hard time dealing with the independence of New Directions. She is off her medications.

2/26 – Betsy is in good spirits, and she is enjoying the New Direction groups.

3/4/2009 - *Well, good morning, it is the middle of the night! I am having trouble sleeping. Oh No! How awful! I went outside for a cigarette. Staff said that it was OK to do that. It's so nice tonight! Spring is in the air! I read the 'Daily Word' on Inner peace. It was a good reading. Betsy's son's birthday is tomorrow 3/5/93. He will be 16 years old. HAPPY BIRTHDAY! Sweet 16! I'm going to lay back down for a while.*

I feel fat, and I need to lose weight from my stomach, butt, legs, thighs. I did my stretching exercises. I have really to stop eating so much. Yuck- ugly feeling! Mmmm coffee, Yum,yum! I luv coffee. Wake up! A brand new day! The sun is rising, and the birds are chirping-SPRING is in the air! I am not eating breakfast, just having coffee, soda, cigarettes and medications. I am determined to lose weight. It has been two weeks since leaving Thornydale Ranch even though I went AWOL twice. I know this is my last chance, and I know I can do this program at New Directions. I want to stay here in recovery and have therapy for my Alcoholism and Mental Health. I will not run away anymore. I need to be here right now. It is a safe place for me to be clean and sober, safe and sane, no danger, no harm to others or myself. I hope to see Mom today. She will have Diet Coke, money, cell phone and huge hugs. She looked nice today. I cashed my $200 check. I locked the money up in the office, and I get $20 per week. With groups and lunch, I feel fat again. I made a store run for those on restrictions. I spent money on 11 items, not bad! St. Patrick Day things: Irish mug, 2 hats, 2 necklaces, candy and snacks - to bring to everyone at home on my 3/17 pass.

I can't wait! I am really looking forward to it. I was counseled that when the cravings and urges to go AWOL and drink occur, I should think of the consequences. Not good. I got money from Project Home. I will be taken to and from my appointments. At this point, I don't think I could make the Suntran bus there and back. The new cell works! Yeah!! I left a recording on Mom's phones. Let's see if she gets the message and calls back??? Tomorrow is my son's birthday. Sweet Sixteen, HAPPY HAPPY HAPPIEST OF THE 16TH BIRTHDAY, Baby!! 3/5/93 I LUV U SON! XXXOOO

3/5/2009 – *I weigh 137 lbs. My favorite station is 96.1 KYPX Rock. My head is killing me. I have a big lump and a huge scab on the back of my head. It really hurts. I feel like I am about to pass out. I have to be excused from group. I got to sleep all morning. It felt good, and I was out like a light. My head really hurts. I am resting and sleeping all day. I am hoping my hurting head gets better. I am praying that the lump goes away and that it is not a skull fracture or something else. I am praying. God, I hope it goes away. My whole head hurts! PAIN!! I need to see a Doctor, but I am afraid of what he would say. I need a shower; maybe that would help. It hurts! I hope Mom answers. Mom is busy. I* *will try to call back in a little while. I finally got through to Mom. She sounds happy. I took the shower but still have a splitting headache.*

3/6/2009 - I feel fat and need to lose weight from my stomach, butt, legs, thighs. I did my stretching exercises. I have really to stop eating so much. Yuck- ugly feeling! Mmmm coffee, Yum,yum! I luv coffee. Wake up! A brand new day! The sun is rising; birds chirping - SPRING is in the air! I am not eating breakfast, just having coffee, soda, cigarettes and medications. I am determined to lose weight. It has been two weeks since leaving Thornydale Ranch even though I went AWOL from New Directions. I know this is my last chance, and I know I can do this program at New Directions. I want to stay here in recovery, therapy for my Alcoholism and Mental Health. I will not run away anymore. I need to be here, right now. It is a safe place for me to be clean, sober, safe and sane. I am in no danger, and I am not a harm to others or myself. I hope to see Mom today. She will have Diet Coke, $, cell phone and huge hugs.

3/5/2009 – I weigh 137 lbs. TGIF – Thank God It's Friday. It's the weekend!! Mom visits on Sunday. Yeah!! I am so proud of my son!

CORE group discussed conflicts – owning one's emotions. Feeling causes thoughts which cause action or response. Cause and effect, actions, beliefs, consequences. I picked up my medications at Fry's with staff. I took a shower, changed my clothes, and the medications are helping me.

3/13 - Betsy's potassium level is critically high. She is glad to be at New Directions after being attacked at Sabino Canyon and Tanque Verde Roads. Her head was cut during the attack. It is not safe for her to be on the streets. It is hard to defend herself at all.

Why I did what I did. What happened? What happened afterwards? I am starting to understand why I did what I did – I ran away. Becoming aware of this, I realize that I ran away due to fear. I think I was afraid. I got scared and went AWOL. A bad thing. I got hurt and had to go to Tucson Medical Center – ER. I don't know who did it or how I got hurt, but it was very scary. It was wrong what happened to me.

A lot has happened since I left Thornydale Ranch. I came to New Directions on 2/18,09. I went to my PCP, and I got a skin test which was negative. So far, I have gone AWOL twice, and I got drunk both times, on Bacardi Lite Dry, Puerto Rican Rum, Hurricane Lager, and 211 Steele Reserve 8.1 % alcohol/vol. I took the # 9 bus from Dodge Bld. and Grant Rd, after visiting the 7-11 on the corner, and I headed East. The first time, I went to Bear Canyon and Catalina Highway. They took me to St. Joseph ER and four-pointed me. They gave me an Ativan and a taxi voucher to the Compass Detox off Dodge. I blew a 2.0 on the Breathalyzer. I sat and waited one hour, drank some water, and then blew a 0 on the Breathalyzer. So they brought me back here to New Directions.

The next time I ran away and went AWOL, I walked down Dodge, past Glenn to Grant, and I stopped at the 7-11. Then I caught the Sun Tran east. Something terrible happened to me out there on Tanque Verde Rd and Sabino Canyon. I got off the bus, went to Walgreens, sat down, drank , went into Walgreens to get some more Bacardi. The next thing I know, I am stumbling and falling, and I found myself in the ladies' room. I am bleeding all over the place. The blood was coming from the back of my head. There were a man and a woman standing there telling me to wait, so I did. The police and paramedics were called - 911. My VINE # from the police states that I have victim rights. I hope they arrest the criminal who hit me. Mom was there. I went to the Tucson

Medical Center Emergency Room. They took pictures of my head.

Then I walked off. I went to Walgreen's and bought a grey sweatshirt because the other one was all bloody, and a hair brush. I went to Dunkin Donuts on Grant. I had some good coffee and donuts. I had money. My head was really hurt, and it still is. Anyhow, thank God, I made it through the night. I slept out with a hospital blanket on the concrete ground in front of the video store. It was cold, and I was shaking . WOW! The next morning, I walked back to Dunkin Donuts and had coffee, cream, sugar, and donuts. I sat, warmed up, and I watched the sunrise. I sat outside of Costco and had 2 Steele reserves 211, Ibuprofen, and MIDOL. My boyfriend wrote on the ground 2007 I LUV U xxxooo. Then I walked to a bus stop and caught the Suntran bus # 9 to Dodge. I walked to New Directions. I've been here ever since.

They moved my room, so they could keep a closer eye on me. I have a single private. My head hurts. I had my medications, dinner, ice with coffee I saved from breakfast. I am going outside to watch the sunset. I have a $200 check from Project HOME, an organization that helps others manage effectively. I'm also waiting on a personal *needs check - $50. MONEY, MONEY, MONEY! I WANT TO SECURE AN APARTMENT SOMEPLACE WHERE I CAN CALL HOME. Yes! An apartment!! I have put on too much weight! I gained a lot. I feel fat!!! Yuck!! It is gross!!! I hate it. I am going on a diet and losing weight. Let's see, right now, I weigh about 145 lbs. - too MUCH! The evening sun is setting, and it's been a good day even though I feel fat. I am sort of craving-having an urge for alcohol right now. Probably because I just talked to Mom, and she really stresses me. I am trying to get a pass for ST. Patrick's Day at home with Mom and the others. I will have 1.5 hours at the house. Mom will pick me up, and we will have corned beef & cabbage- sounds good!*

I was told this is my last chance. I ran away twice. They might ask me to leave. I want to stay and work the program. I want recovery and therapy. I want to rent an apartment and live there. In this program, New Directions, there are a lot of people struggling with worse problems: using, drinking, drugging, other issues different from me. I am here to work on myself and my issues in recovery here. I will have been here two weeks. God, I luv u, son the mother of our son, Sweet 16 birthday! I am very,

*very proud of you, son, and yes, you are fine,
doing excellent in everything that you really
are! We love you. Your mother, Elizabeth.
An AA meeting, medications, wrap up, lights
out coming up. I am drinking Diet Shasta
Cola and going outside to smoke. I wish that
I had better medicine, ...God, that Bacardi
and lager was good! Too bad somebody
fucked me up- they hurt me! I like my drinks.
I need to get a house- an apartment or home.
I want to live at home −Thinking about
drinking, cravings and urges. This too shall
pass. I luv u son! Don't worry, Smile and Be
Happy! Xxxxoooo
Good meeting! Speaker Bill, another Dan
(remember from Kino psych unit) was there.
Sometimes sitting for that long of a time is
hard for me. I get impatient. I left, and then
came back again. I hope to get a good night's
sleep. I've been up all day and I'm very tired.
After wrap up, I'll smoke one more, change
clothes, then pray. I need sleep, no more
'stinkin' thinkin' about drinkin'. Not right now.
I am too close to getting my own place.
Apartment, maybe, (studio, efficiency), I
have over $2000 at Project HOME. I am
seeing mom (NEPM) for lunch St. Pat's Day.
This week, Mom cashed my check for Diet
Coke, Pantene, cell phone Verizon (one that*

works, I hope). I pray for sleep. Good day: Courage, faith, experience, strength today. We'll make it dear, God bless.

3/7/2009 - Going to have a great day today. I read the 'Daily Word.' It felt good to rest and sleep all day.

3/8/2009 — I had strange dreams. I can't wait for Mom and Rebecca to visit. I am looking forward to seeing them. It was a good, good visit! I am going to cuddle all night with nice warm blankets. I had a good day!! The little pitter-patter of raindrops sounds neat! Spring is really here. April showers bring May flowers.

3/9/2009 - Good morning, I am feeling good, and I hope to have a nice day today. I will take a shower. I had strange dreams. Maybe the storm will clear up and we will have sunshine and blue skies. I need lab work. They saved a dinner for me. It was a really good meeting and day!

3/10/2009 — I weigh 140 lbs. I am calling Mom. I am not going to be writing for a while. Signing off, I luv u, EBM. Serenity Prayer: God grant me the serenity to accept the things I cannot change; courage to change the things I can; and the wisdom to know the difference.

3/19 - Betsy is at New Directions. She is less confused and more involved. She is engaging in groups, learning and making progress. She has Been at New Directions for 30 days. She is now off restriction and is allowed to leave with another client. She is much less shy, and she is interacting.

> *I came back to New Directions and feel that this is a safe place for me to be. It is a good program. I feel the need to be here in recovery and therapy. The groups, classes, and meetings are very helpful and good. I really want to stay in the program here. I think I can do it. When I leave New Directions, I will be prepared to go out into the world. I would like to get and rent an apartment – a studio or an efficiency when I leave. For now, though, I really really feel the need to be here at New Directions in recovery, having therapy for Substance Abuse and Mental Health. I am dedicated and completely compliant with my recovery here in the program. I am totally committed and would go to any lengths to stay clean and sober, continuing in recovery for Substance Abuse and Mental Health.*

3/23 – Betsy needs a new place as the program is not fit for her. They cannot keep her safe. It was her 3rd time relapsing, and she will be leaving New

Directions. Betsy is fixated on leaving Compass treatment.

3/24 – Betsy went for walk. She is scared of staff. She disappeared and blew it. She is not allowed on the premises if intoxicated. She is on an unknown substance, not alcohol. So she was taken to Compass. All female B&C. She relapsed twice in two days.

She was in front of Compass, smoking and causing trouble. She could not understand why she was brought here. She was kicked out of New Directions because of the relapse. She is not allowed to return. She went to Compass for detox, but she did not remember how she got there. She is extremely confused. She refuses to sign in, but she finally did. She was taken to B&C where all her belongings were.

3/26 - Betsy was drunk when her Case Manager went to pick her up. She was slurring and stumbling. There was an alcohol smell. She was helped to bed and was up all night. She did not take her meds.

3/27 – She was unconscious on the couch. After knocking on door and ringing the bell, she answered and was disoriented. She did not know where she was. She took all her meds for 2 weeks. She was brought to the hospital and could barely walk. She was mumbling but did not smell like alcohol. She was transported to a 24 hour facility. She was compliant.

3/30 – She does not know the date.

3/31 – She has overtaken her medications. She cannot walk. She has low energy and is slurring. At the hospital she was very slow. She was admitted to Tucson Medical Center.

4/1 - She was at the Crisis Bed last night. She had no refills left of Hydroxyzine, Lorazepam, Depakote, or Trazodone. She agreed to go to a new 30 day program at Casa De Vida. Her mother is worried about her not eating. Her Case Manager reminded her that she had had 189 days sober and that she could try again. She did not answer when asked what her biggest obstacle was. She was given a Group list at LaFrontera Center. Betsy was moving very slowly. She did eat, but her hands were a little shaky. She needs to detox from abusing meds. She felt rejected when she was kicked out of the New Directions Program for Women, having gone there after the hospital. She stated that she was tired. She walked and moved slowly.

4/2 - Betsy participated in discussion. What can she get out of Recovery: family, jobs, freedom, peace of mind, pay bills, buy things.

4/3 - Going to the Lab for blood work, she was walking very slowly. Her Case Manager got McDonald's for her. Afterwards, she was walking faster and was more talkative. She had more insight.

PSYCH REPORTS

4/6 – She appears over-sedated: will discontinue Depakote, Trazodone, Hydroxyzine; continue Lorazepam, Trihexyphenidyl, Campral, Fluphenazine Decanoate. She is tired and sad.

4/7 - Betsy has been out of meds. She had not picked up her meds. She was appreciative of her Case Manager taking scripts to pharmacy, BUT she refused. She needs to put pills in med boxes. Betsy was pacing and seems anxious. The nurse had to staff with CPSA.

4/8 - Betsy still has problems with getting meds. She gets Lorazepam only every 2 weeks when she gets an injection. Her med box was packed. She has been out of meds for a few days.

4/9 - She has been sleeping a lot. She is talkative, often repeating herself. She is anxious which shows in her body language and expressions. She will eat if others eat with her. She is anxious: drinking excessive diet cola which suppresses appetite. She was recently in the hospital for overtaking medications. She relapsed with alcohol. Still has urges to drink, struggles to stay sober. Shared in group about her past with alcohol.

4/10 - Does not follow through on attending Groups. Too tired.

4/14 - Gets blurred vision from Lorazepam. Very harsh with Case Manager, wanted to do her own thing.

4/20 - Court Ordered Treatment. Waiting for approval for CDV(treatment center). PSYCH REPORT-

Not medically cleared to enter CDV because of Potassium and Sodium levels. She is high in Sodium and Potassium. Ana's House Bed and Breakfast evicted her for: smoking in house, not high enough functioning, stereo 'lost' (probably took it for boyfriend who is homeless and living in desert; often confused, often sedated, unable to walk straight. Smelled of alcohol)

4/21- SERVICE PLAN: Attend five groups a week. She is still having problems getting medications.

4/23 - Betsy did not understand reason for being evicted. Options: move home with Mother or B&C on East side.

4/24 - Hit by truck last night who drove off. At the University Medical Center ER, Betsy was impatient waiting to have her broken left femur treated. She was crossing at Grant and Swan against the light which was flashing yellow. She was charged with being wrong. She took one Percoset and felt better.

4/27- Betsy has to leave B&C because of a conflict with other resident over alcohol. She is confused and is overtaking meds. She walked to ER because of being in a lot of pain. Got full arm cast. Said she was sick of having La Frontera Center control her life, and she is not interested in attending any appointments. Even after Case Manager explained it was a medical appointment so that her bones could heal healthily to avoid infection. Betsy ended conversation abruptly and did not want to talk to CM. She was angry and defensive feeling that the Case Manager was imposing on her.

4/28 - Betsy not willing to look at new B&Cs with Case Manager. She got two bus passes to go to a medical appointment. She did not remember overtaking her Lorazepam last week or getting filled med box. She had run out of Percoset, 40 pills worth. She was urged to stay for group, but she said she was tired and wanted to go home.

4/29 - Betsy continues to drink, abuse meds, and she needs to utilize coping skills to deal with stressors.

4/30 - At the ER, her Blood Alcohol Level was .136, twice the legal limit. She is abusing medications and alcohol.

5/1 - Betsy did go to her doctor's appointment for her arm. She is groggy. Wondering if she is abusing pain medications. She is at a new B&C where she took all her medications. She went to the 24 hour crisis bed at Sonora House, but she went AWOL after going to the ER. She is moving very slow and is having a hard time getting up and moving. She could not remember yesterday's events, and she wants to go to CDV.

5/5 - Her mother taking her out to eat for Cinco de Mayo

5/10 - Crisis Line call that Betsy left B&C and had not returned, not saying where going.

5/11 - Drank, rode bus, slept on streets, woke up, drank more, walked to TMC ER; released to B&C, cannot go to CDV until arm is healed.

5/12 - Betsy was denied Lorazepam and Campral, due to drinking and overusing medications. She will take Artane for side effects. She has a cold and pain. She doesn't feel well enough to attend group. Her mother is out of town. She is confused about weekend events. She is sluggish and has a hoarse voice.

5/13 – She is out of meds and denied taking too many at one time.

5/19 - She is feeling badly and is not going to the SSA office with her Case Manager as planned.

The House of Heart Era

5/20 – Betsy has moved to the **House of Heart**. She likes B&C because it's 'like a mansion; one of the nicest places I have lived.' She has strong cravings, but walks, smokes, watches TV and talks to family. She is still interested in CDV, and she seemed better.

5/26 - Her mother took her to court and paid her fines. She would repay her from SSI money. She attended group. From 5/23-25 she went to COMPASS because she felt she was 'going off the deep end,' and she felt she had no one to talk to. So she had a beer. She went into detox. She feels better and is stable. She wants to attend RP group. Her Case Manager would take her. We made the suggestion that she go to Thornydale Ranch while waiting for CDV, but she said instead she wanted OP and to go to groups, to not drink alcohol, and to take her medications correctly. If not she would consider Thornydale Ranch. She lost 17 lbs. in the last few months. She said she was overfed at The Ranch. She was refused her request for Lorazepam and Campral because of overtaking them. She attended a morning anger management group. She shared experiences and offered support.

5/28 - She attended RP. She shared about struggling with cravings. She wants to remain sober.

6/2 – She attended the morning group. She read aloud and shared a story of forgiveness. She offered support to others.

6/4 - RP grp. She shared about her dual diagnosis and the benefits of being sober. She refused a ride to group because she feels too sick to come.

6/11- Psych Report: Betsy took Vicodin 50 tablets in addition to her Percoset. She needs to be in a medical facility because she represents Danger to Self. Her speech is slurred, and she has tangential and illogical thought processes. She is disoriented, smells of alcohol, and is staggering around the courtyard. She is unfocused and is laying down on the sidewalk, near parking lot. She is tired. While waiting for her mother, she was mumbling negative things about La Frontera Center staff. When she walked outside to smoke, she agreed to go to Compass. She would be revoked on COT and would have to go to Kino Hospital. She fell asleep in the lobby chair, and she could not stay awake. She was very subdued, barely responding. She would not wait at Compass and declined services.

6/18 - Mother would not take her to pharmacy to get her pain meds (narcotics).

6/23- She is confused. Her stomach hurts from ulcers.

6/26 – Betsy is not wearing her brace, and her arm is not setting. She is against going to Thornydale Ranch.

6/29 – Her mother told us that the Betsy left B&C and may have gone to the ER on June 28. Her mother is planning an involuntary Petition as the Court Ordered Treatment is expiring.

7/7 - At the Ranch: Betsy was dropped off at La Frontera Center but she wandered off and was gone for an hour with her ex-boyfriend who is a bad influence. She said she went for a walk. She is paranoid and defensive when asked to speak with the supervisor. She refused to return to the Ranch and to go to the nurse for injection. She got on the bus with ex-boyfriend.

7/8 - The police brought her back for her injection, but she kept leaving. She only talked about her arm and ulcer pain. She wanted her pain meds. Her mother called the police in an attempt to locate her. She has abrasions on her face, arms, elbows and a lump on her forehead. She vomited after getting her shot. She had to be medically cleared to return to Thornydale Ranch. Her Case Manager volunteered to take her to TMC. She seemed intoxicated by speech and behavior. She was medically cleared and returned to Thornydale Ranch.

7/9 - At the ART meeting, the Betsy said she enjoyed Thornydale Ranch. She wished to stay there and finish up treatment. She went AWOL to see someone special to her. She knows she made a mistake and promises she won't do it again. If she goes AWOL, she would lose her bed at Thornydale Ranch. She has a tentative discharge in 3 months. She wants the medications she lost .

7/11 - Could not go to the community outing, did all chores, attended all groups and barn group. She worked on socialization.

7/15 – Betsy's SERVICE PLAN: Attend 5 groups a week; get medical approval to attend CDV; has been sober 2 wks.

7/24 – She is afraid to go out after dark, and so is not attending NA/AA mtgs.

7/25 – She walked out of Thornydale Ranch, called taxi, not Court Ordered Treatment. She was seen by other clients. She is crying, feeling sorry for self.

7/27- She was medically cleared at North West (NW) Hospital ER and she will be allowed back. She was verbally abusive, "I hate X for making me do this."

7/30 – She was transported to doctor's appointment for arm. She was agitated before and after. She refused to go to group. She is struggling with cravings for alcohol, 'I have to fight these cravings every day'. She is also anxious.

7/31- She left group. She refused to find support about writing a crisis and safety plan.

8/2- She kept leaving and returning to group. She is preoccupied with next medications. She has problems focusing on the present and on next events.

8/3 - She said Staff at Thornydale Ranch were mad at her for using bad language. Her arm is healing ok, but she feels 'scarred for life'.

8/5 – She is enjoying her time at Thornydale Ranch. It is more structured and there are better groups. She has too few points to go on Mt. Lemmon outing.

8/6 - In group participation she takes feedback and confrontations.

8/7 – She completed Crisis and Safety Plan.

8/9 – She rushes to consume medications and has as many as possible.

8/10 - 'I know that everyone is talking about me.' She demanded to have her cash given to her from the medical closet. She was denied because of AWOL history. She is not participating and desire to leave

Thornydale Ranch. She is angry with staff and shows a lack of responsibility.

8/11 - ART meeting with Mother. She will go to two AA and NA meetings per week. She will work on habit if interrupting others, and she will stay for entire group instead of leaving early. She is angry at missing the weekend outing and interrupted each who spoke. She used harsh language with and yelled at Mother about money. She did apologize to Mother, and she agreed to work on kinder ways of expressing her emotions. She is not doing chores, but other ADL's. Discharge date is moved back to 12/4. She deflects responsibility and blames it on her arm. She told her mother that when she brings food and soda, there is less incentive to complete chores, etc. to gain points to go to the store.

8/13 - Mother going out of town is usually a 'trigger'. It's hard for her to sleep.

8/15 - She has a problem with caffeinated beverages and swallowed all of it addictively at cut off time.

8/17 – She may get out of arm brace soon.

8/18 – She is hiding caffeine in her room and is verbally abusive to staff. When she appears angry, she says, 'Go to hell'.

8/20 – During the medical appointment, she said "I am going to the bathroom," and we could not find her in the smoking area either. AWOL

8/21 – Tucson Police Department found her last night slurring words. She was medically cleared at

St Mary's Hospital (SMH)to return to Thornydale Ranch. She had a bottle of Benadryl in her purse. She overdosed on alcohol in a public place.

8/22 – She lacks motivation to do chores, eat breakfast, and lunch. She is anxious, not able to sit still.

8/24 - Her sister met her at the appointment. 'I feel much better having my sister here to support me'.

8/24 - " I want to continue residing at Thornydale Ranch & follow their programs to learn to live independently in the community.' Needs a sustained willingness & patience for TR environment.

8/25 – I left group. "I am too stressed to be here right now and need a PRN".

8/27- Profanity and agitation with clients and staff.

8/31- In the morning. Betsy said, 'I think that I have finally learned my lesson this time, and I'm doing much better." At an La Frontera Center appointment, her demeanor and attitude changed from enjoying the radio to immediate agitation and negative attitude. She said, 'MT ROSE and Thornydale Ranch are a terrible place.' Then she had a conversation with herself: 'I'm just going to leave. Nancy, you cannot stop me." She continued to berate staff for watching where she went. She was paranoid. Her boyfriend was outside. She handed him money and cigarettes. She began to cry and say "I love you." She was verbally berating Thornydale Ranch in the La Frontera Center lobby. She complained to a nurse about staff at TR and how they followed her. She reviewed injustices done to her since she was 16 yrs. She said she felt old and angry. She wanted to speak with her Recovery facilitator (RF). She went outside and met her boyfriend again. She went AWOL. She is no longer Court Order Treatment, and so she cannot be revoked. Seeing her boyfriend must have triggered her impulse to walk off. She told him "I have a $65 check." She debated about walking to Circle K on Craycroft. I asked her to stay on the property. She said, "You can't make me." I asked her boyfriend to convince her to stay. His response was, "Get out of our way. She is my wife. Don't follow us. You won't survive in the neighborhoods." I watched them walk away and called Thornydale Ranch. Thornydale Ranch would call the Residential Supervisor. I waited 10 minutes to see if she returned, and then I returned to Thornydale Ranch.

9/2 - Betsy was arrested for littering, and she was charged with Drinking in Public(DIP). On the Mental Health Unit, we had a meeting with Judge Friday. Betsy was quiet and introverted. For CDV there is a month's WL –Wait List. CPSA sent Notification of Incarcerated Member to Criminal Justice. Case Aide verified Betsy was 'in custody'. Her current medical sheet and most recent psychiatric note will be sent.

9/11- Someone does not feel Court Ordered Treatment is needed. She cannot return to

Thornydale Ranch. She should go to B&C. Someone wants to drop petition.

9/18 – She is at La Frontera Center with her mother. She suggested that Betsy stay for groups. Betsy declined and said she was 'too tired'. She was encouraged not to always have excuses, to just follow through, and to go to groups. She was given the Warmline and LEC Crisis line numbers if her drinking is triggered, and she needs to talk with someone. She is scheduled with her Case Manager at 8:30 for check in. Her mother went over boundaries now that Betsy is no longer under Court Order Treatment and in B&C.

9/24 – Betsy met with the hospital liaison who reported that Betsy was having a hard time not being able to smoke or drink caffeine, both of which make her symptoms worse. As Betsy said, they are 'not good for my recovery.' When she asked for petition to be dropped, she said she would be willing to do anything OP. She said she would also be COT compliant as well. She is not hearing voices, and she is stabilizing but anxious.

9/30 - During group she drank some liquid medications, but she refused to show what she drank. She is angry and needs a substance abuse group. It has been hard for her to say, 'no' to housemates who ask for things. In a new group, she observed, as she was new. She drank a lot of liquid medication. In her RP group, she listened but did not share.

10/1 – Betsy moved out of B&C. She could not get to La Frontera Center in time for Doctor's appointment.

10/14 - PSYCH REPORT: Betsy was recently discharged from the hospital for mood changes, psychosis, and alcohol abuse. Her medications include: Ambien for insomnia; Trihexyphenidyl for akathisia; Diphenhydramine for restlessness; Fluphenazine for psychosis; Trazodone for insomnia; Lorazepam for muscle tension.

10/15 – At St. Joseph's Hospital, Betsy is disorganized and disoriented in the ER. She drank last night, and her meds are missing. She is not eating. She is not SI. Her medications are missing. She is not eating and is confused.

10/16 – She is psychotic. She has a problem sitting still and following directions. She is not able to think clearly. She told bizarre stories and had hallucinations. For example, she said, 'I had a teenager in that bag.' She was anxious and constantly fidgeting. She picked scabs until they bled. DP. The Betsy said, "I'll be glad when this world is over on the day I die." She was transported to Sonora Shelter.

11/2 – Betsy denied overtaking meds despite not having any left.

11/11 - PSYCH REPORT: Betsy is doing well.

11/23 - Betsy is going to her mother's house for Thanksgiving.

12/9- PSYCH REPORT : A OK

12/23 – Betsy was transferred to Mountain La Frontera Center despite not wanting to be transferred there.

12/26 - Betsy called for bridge and was denied from SAMHC.

2010

1/7 - PSYCHIATRIST APPOINTMENT (MONTHLY) and lasts 20 minutes. She felt mentally stable on current medications. She had no side effects: Fluphenazine Decanoate-25mg, an injection every two weeks, for mood stability and psychosis prevention; Lorazepam, 1mg PRN, for restlessness and muscle tension; Trihexyphenidyl, 5mg BID, for Akathisia.

Mental status: alert, fully oriented, euthymic mood, expressive, and appropriate affect. Not recurrent thoughts of death, suicide or harm others. Not psychotic, and her insight and judgment are good.

DIAGNOSIS: Axis 1 Schizoaffective Disorder; Alcohol Dependence; Nicotine Dependence; Eating Disorder, NOS : reports eating regular schedule

1/20 – She is taking 25 mg of Prolixin in her left hip. She is not showing any side effects. The Prolixin controls her mental illness symptoms. Betsy could not say what those symptoms are. When she relapsed in past, she lost her home and other material possessions. She could not list symptoms related to relapse. She denies ever hearing voices, being paranoid, or having strange thoughts. Betsy said that she has only suffered from depression. Her mood was euthymic; affect congruent; speech loud; thoughts organized; and she was clean and appropriately dressed.

1/21- Betsy called: She is getting kicked out of Board and Care(B&C). She is requesting a new home because she relapsed over weekend and then came back drunk. The House Manager (HM) took her to COMPASS, and she spent the weekend there. She admits to addiction and struggles every day. We suggested residential Substance Abuse (SA) treatment, but Betsy preferred Outpatient groups (OP) and she said she would start going. HM stated Betsy had problems with medication management, and she often takes more than prescribed. We suggested that Betsy return to the Thornydale Ranch, as she learned some really good skills that helped her. Betsy agreed, and so her case manager (CM) completed a Thornydale Ranch packet and is prepared to help find a new B&C.

1/22 - Betsy stated that she went with her friend and his brother and stayed out all night with them. She blacked out and lost all her money. She likes her new B&C, and she feels safe there. 'I feel healthy and I am taking care of myself'. She admitted to having cravings. She said that she can call people, and she smokes with her roommate. She has not been journaling. She watches TV, listens to the radio, or goes for walks. She wants to work outside in the yard. She agreed to come to Eastside La Frontera groups and to consider Nueva Luz (NL). She asked about Our Place Clubhouse because she wants independent living eventually, a long term goal. She needs to not drink, and she needs to take her meds, keep her appointments, and follow the house rules. She wants to stay out of the hospital and court-ordered treatment (COT). She likes her B&C. The owner reminded Betsy about rules: if she comes home drunk, she would be kicked out.

2/17 – Betsy's behavior is not her usual. She is loud and irritable one moment, and then she whispers, putting her finger to her lips to quiet herself. Sometimes she giggles inappropriately, being silly. Then she turns quite serious. She says her meds are monitored. Her mood and affect are inappropriate and labile. Her thoughts are organized. She is clean but her hair is dirty and uncombed. She is casually dressed. We updated her Service and Crisis plans. Betsy declines SA groups. She appears distracted and confused, staring off and losing track of conversation. She has poor insight.

3/2 – She loves living at the HOH, and she is looking towards independent living. Her mood is cheerful; affect bright; speech and thoughts rapid; clean and neatly dressed.

Psych and Medical report: Axis 3 Liver Disease, Weight loss

Reports: Betsy is doing well except that Trazodone is too sedating. She wakes up groggy. Will lower the dose to 50mg. She likes Naltrexone to reduce cravings.

3/16 – We discussed her medications, her past noncompliance, and her need for injection over oral med. She is doing much better in the B&C as medications are in med boxes and monitored daily. Her mood is cheerful; affect congruent; speech and thoughts organized but somewhat evasive. She is disheveled with inadequate hygiene.

3/25 – Betsy expressed a medical concern. There are not enough refills until her next appointment . The concern was forwarded to the nurse for review and coordination of care. She is slurring with slow but loud speech .

4/1- HM locked up money, cigarettes, soda, and medications. Betsy feels intimidated. She has been threatened with eviction. The HM accuses her of stealing and misusing meds.

4/13 - Naltrexone helping with cravings. I asked about New Life with social outings, bowling and cookouts. CM would go with her until she felt comfortable.

4/19-22 She wants to move out of the B&C because she feels the restrictions are galling. She feels the HM is selling her cigarettes to others. There is conflict. A

Case aide assessed the quality of care in the B&C, and she approved the care.

4/26 - Betsy says residents gossip and blame her for things, and she is fed up with it.

4/28 – She seemed anxious (body, language, voice). RF Service Plan Meeting goal: To address SA and learn basic skills to be a valuable member of society. When having a hard time, she said she wants to communicate with staff and use her coping skills, to take meds as prescribed and learn what they are for, to be clean and sober from alcohol, and to receive NL services.

5/10 PSYCH REPORT: She is having problems falling asleep. She has been drinking too many caffeinated beverages. She has agreed to an increase of Trazodone and to lower caffeine. She has had no alcohol for 6 months.

6/10 PSYCH REPORT: No alcohol for 7 months. She is losing weight and now weighs 110 lbs. and is 5'9". RF-Service Plan Meeting (same as before). She went for a tour of NL.

6/14- Betsy was evicted from House of Heart for relapsing. She went to Kino Hospital, Safe Haven, and then to Compass.

6/20 – Betsy went to a different B&C.

6/25 – The hospital dropped mother's petition requesting that Betsy's primary health issues are SA related. She was discharged from Kino Hospital, and she was out of meds. She went to the New Directions women's SA treatment center.

6/26 – She left the B&C to pick up meds and never returned.

7/8 – Betsy is in Kino Hospital. She was with her boyfriend when he was assaulted. She went to see him in the hospital. She was arrested for littering, trespassing, alcohol use, and was taken to jail for a week. Betsy was homeless, and then taken to Kino Hospital. She can be discharged if Betsy is stable which means reaching a 'baseline'. She still needs Court Ordered Treatment. She will be placed in La Frontera Center until Monday, and then, OP team, and then back. Betsy was cooperative and compliant for the hearing.

7/15- Betsy was placed on Court Ordered Treatment for 3 months. She is impatient waiting for transportation.

7/28 - Criminal Justice Liaison needs the compliance report from CM. The charges were dismissed. She is not in custody.

8/10- B&C reports Betsy drinks as soon as she gets her weekly money from Project HOME. Betsy is irritated and denies it. Then she stated if she kept drinking she could not 'handle it' and would be out on the streets.

8/18 – She weighs 117 lbs. with her clothes on. It is hard for her to gain weight. She drinks Ensure. She likes Sunday breakfasts with her mother at Village

Inn. She is very happy, easy, comfortable, and engaging with interesting conversation. She likes her B&C, her relationship with the Home Manager, and her mother.

8/25 – She overtook medications to be able to fall asleep. She denied it was a Suicide Attempt. Though she said that 'it was a lot of meds.' She is aware of the risk of hurting herself. She is not sad or depressed, but she is not eating. In Tucson Medical Center she was lethargic, without expression. She denied that it was a suicide attempt.

8/26 – The House Manager said 14 pills were taken by the Betsy. Betsy was not oriented, and she was sedated. She agreed to go to the hospital. Her speech is slurred, and she is sedated. She minimized what happened.

8/27- Betsy was taken to Tucson Medical Center twice in one week for medicine overuse. She called five times for refills and was revoked. She was not complying with COT treatment. Betsy stayed at Casa Alegre for the weekend. She was concerned about not having her medication, but because of overmedicating, she was not given a 'bridge'. She agreed that if she began to withdraw and start to feel sick, she should inform staff to take her to the ER.

8/30 - We quashed Revocation and put in a 'Medical Bridge' instead. She was transported to East Clinic.

9/1 – Her HM reported that Betsy was drinking last night and that she did not come home. Betsy admitted to taking all of her medications. The Coordinator said Betsy had to keep 9/1 appointment or she would be revoked. Betsy showed signs of intoxication: slow speech; eyes and face drooping; smelled of alcohol.

9/2 - PSYCH REPORT-Could benefit from long term dual diagnosis treatment facility.

9/16 – Betsy lost her wallet and then found it. It was returned to LFC. She weighed 120 lbs., and she seemed future-oriented, clean, and social.

9/27 - HM reports mood swings, anger, sneaking to pharmacy to get Lorazepam, her prescription medication.

9/30 – Betsy was loud, used slow speech, and was possibly intoxicated from an unknown substance.

10/1 – Betsy seemed groggy, spoke slowly, and did not smell like alcohol.

10/7 – Betsy wants to be off COT and to be medically cleared.

10/8 - Betsy felt healthy, clean, and liking her second chance at life. She does not like waking up in the ER.

10/12 - Mother states that Betsy gives her boyfriend money and cigarettes on a daily basis. He can be psychotic and violent, but he has not been violent with Betsy. She is worried that Anna's B&C will be labeled a 'drug house' and then shut down.

10/21 – Betsy is showing improvement and functioning better. Her mood is stable and is not showing depression or anxiety.

11/5 - Betsy is intoxicated. She smells of beer, and her dress is messy. Her grooming is fair. Her eyes are glassed over.

11/16 – Betsy reports that SA groups help her abstain from alcohol. She said she also needs a good support network, to stop hanging out with old friends, and to stay medication stable. She said she plans to attend groups. She said, "I love my family." Her sister turned 50; she is 48. She is smiling, soft-spoken, maintaining good eye contact, casually dressed in jeans, sweatshirt, and a down vest.

12/14 - She is compliant. She is anxious about court. At the City Court Hearing her Case Manager helped Betsy put in an application for Mental Health Diversion. Betsy smelled like alcohol, and the judge said that next time she will give a Breathalyzer test. The judge also said that by January 11, 2011 Betsy will need proof of attending SA groups. Betsy relapsed and was cited for drinking in public.

12/20 - Betsy is too tired from injection to attend group.

Very end of December, 2010 - End of year service plan meeting. Betsy needs to attend groups: Relapse Prevention, SA Education, Empowering Women, Building and Maintaining Positive Relationships, Wellness Management and Recovery. Betsy shared in her group meeting about losing her trailer from drinking, having had a good Thanksgiving, and about using her spiritual tools for recovery.

2011

Very beginning of January, 2011 - Betsy discussed personal problems with past relationship and how it affects her now. She has difficulty processing some emotions, and she is open for group feedback. She discussed a plan for relapse prevention. She is still working on getting over broken relationships which all centered around drugs and alcohol. She said, 'Everyone I know uses a chemical to get by.' Peers gave her advice.

1/7 – Betsy was actively listening. She shared how she got through hard times during the holidays.

1/14 – Betsy showed signs of intoxication. She participated but was disruptive.

1/28 – Betsy appears to be intoxicated. She had family issues as a child, and she said that it is hard for her to stop drinking alcohol. She is wearing clean but dirty and stained clothing. but her mood and affect are cheerful. Her thoughts are organized and relevant. She weighs127 lbs. She needs to attend 36 hours of classes before her February 14, 2011 court hearing. She is staying away from her boyfriend who always drinks. She has to attend groups sober. She refused to come to the office to discuss sobriety during groups. She is in denial and is making excuses.

2/3 - Betsy stated she was a long term alcoholic and is emotionally shut down. She stated that when she used drugs she did not react as others do

2/10 - Betsy does not even know where to start in explaining why she relapses. In the past, she blamed it on someone or an event; this time she will try to work the program.

2/14 – A private social worker with an attorney's office will take Betsy to the court hearing. Betsy did not attend. The hearing was reset for 3/21/11. She must attend, or there will be a warrant for her arrest.

2/17 - Betsy states that our society is a 'a drug based society.' They give a pill to go to sleep and one to wake you up. She mentioned all the addictive medications that cause cravings for street drugs.

2/18 - Betsy praying to remain sober, and she is thankful for having her parents in her life. She appeared under the influence with glassy eyes, slurring speech, and slow walking.

2/25 – She likes The House of Heart (B&C) and wants to make amends to her family. She shared how difficult it is dealing with her MI in addition to alcoholism.

3/11 – Betsy shared about spending time with her family. She felt ill and left the group early.

3/28 – She reported doing well. She doesn't like groups. It is hard to sit still and to listen to others' problems. She was reminded about MH Diversion and about having to answer to the judge about not attending groups. She said she would go. She avoids working on her recovery from SA. She is cheerful and then sad. She talked about not liking groups, and then she laughed immediately after.

4/13 - Betsy is getting kicked out of the B&C for stealing food and blankets to give to her homeless boyfriend. She needs to find a new B&C, and she got a list. The HM has to travel, and she doesn't trust Betsy enough to leave her alone in the house.

4/15 - Betsy gives her clothes to boyfriend too. She missed the court date, and has not attended groups.

4/21 - Betsy says she has relapsed so many times that it is hard to come back. She is trying to avoid triggers, but they are everywhere.

4/22 – Betsy appeared sedated with minimal participation.

4/25 – Betsy weighs 120 lbs. She attended SMART recovery group, and she is improving hygiene.

4/27 – Betsy has been enjoying spending time with her mother. She is paying attention, both her eye movement and her body language.

4/29 – During SA Education, Betsy shared about using breathing exercises to relax. Betsy was grateful for doing well.

5/2 - Attended Empowering Women group-on time, eager to participate, first time, & shared about self, been involved with LFC since early '80's;shared thoughts about the quotes, enjoyed what peers said, & nodded head while they were talking.

5/3 – Betsy told her peers that she thinks about drinking every day and understands the strong urge to try just one drink. She 'is the expert on relapse prevention' and has all the information. But she falls down when she tries to put it into action. She was engaged in discussion, actively read with the group, and was supportive of peers

5/11 – Betsy came for 10 minutes. She handed in a paper to be signed and then left. She did not return.

5/20 – Betsy appeared much more engaged in group, and she told everyone that she needed to come to group. She said that most drugs she can experiment with and leave, but alcohol is a serious problem for her. She shared that she had been hospitalized.

5/24 – Betsy was engaged and she participated. She was supportive and respectful of peers.

5/26 – She talked about chances you take after you get high on drugs. Safe sex is forgotten. It is hard to stay focused on safety when you use drugs. This information will make you think about yourself and your partner.

5/27 – She shared about dealing with stress by walking, listening to music, writing in her journal. SERVICE PLAN: Betsy signed a Judicial Review form. She is doing well. She had not seen her boyfriend for a while. She looked sad. I suggested that she did well by trying to help him and that now she should concentrate on herself by keep coming to groups and taking care of herself. She agreed. I praised her for doing well and for attending the Anger Management Group today. She was in a happy mood, wearing clean clothes, and improving.

6/1 – Betsy was very engaged in group, supportive towards others, and involved in material presented.

6/2 – She talked about her long struggle to stay sober. She said she will always fight her desire to drink. She said she is staying busy helping her parents.

6/9 – She is tearful as she told how drinking has ruined her relationship with her parents. She does not lives in a B&C because her parents do not trust her anymore. Alcohol has made her financially poor and physically unhealthy.

6/14 – She was supportive of peers and engaged in activity.

Late June, 2010 – PSYCH REPORT - Her gait is unsteady. Her speech is slurred. She said she is tired. She could have been drinking. She has limited insight and judgment. Her weight is down, but denies that it is an issue.

7/5 – SA Education group. She shared how she has stopped using street drugs and has been much better since then.

8/5 - During the EW group, they watched 'Fried Green Tomatoes' and discussed how women were treated then and how they are treated now.

Betsy: I 'am a mother of an 18 year old boy who was adopted at age eighteen months because I was a bad

Mommy.' Betsy befriended a peer and shared similar stories of losing their children.

SERVICE PLAN: Want to improve my self-esteem: think negatively at least 1x per 2 wks.

8/5 – SA Education. Topic: Stress and Negative Emotions; identified strengths; skills to manage and reframe stressors.

8/9 – Betsy watched 'The Soloist' and was engaged. She gave very insightful responses to discussion questions.

8/10 - First Group Counseling: Topic - Love is a Choice. Betsy was quiet and respectful. She made appropriate interactions, and she fell asleep.

8/11- SA Education. The discussion was about craving, dopamine, and how it relates to relapse. Betsy had very difficult time. She was loud and was disruptive talking to herself. She had a hard time tracking conversations. Poor participation.

8/12 - SA Education – Discussed relapse process: from triggers, to thoughts, to cravings, to relapse.

8/15 – Betsy said she had a 'nice weekend and slept a lot' because of the rainy weather and the medications. Betsy said that shots of Prolixin help her a lot. She said she enjoys movies and believes that she is more independent than women in 'Fried Green Tomatoes.'

8/17 - Second Grp C: Discussed Power of Forgiveness and the 5 steps to heal painful interactions when you feel hurt or betrayed. Betsy was quiet, and polite. She made appropriate interactions with little or no participation.

8/18 - Relapse: We discussed skills to avoid strategies, how brain functions in relationship to triggers and cravings, and how to start over. Peers offered encouragement to stay sober.

8/19 - Betsy had a good day. She is doing well at House of Heart.

8/22 - Betsy enjoys swimming, long walks, writing in journal, and watching TV. She really enjoys HOH.

8/24 - Group C: Discussed mistakes to avoid during conflict resolution. Avoid: lumping everything together; being defensive; over generalizing; insisting on being right; mind-reading; 'psychoanalyzing'; forgetting to listen; blaming; trying to win.

Betsy shared that she had learned to do something good for myself, family, friends, and to others. She will take better care of self by not being stressed, being anxious, panicking being at peace, helping others, being on best behavior. Betsy shared last week's activities that helped to improve her relationship with herself.

8/25 – Betsy stated 'not feeling well,' and she contributed little group participation.

8/26 – She shared about doing well and getting along with her family.

8/29 – She shared how much she enjoys where she lives and how she is honoring her values. She started her Vision Board.

8/31 - Group C Topic: How to build positive boundaries and make wise decisions. Betsy engaged in the discussion, and she interacted appropriately with peers.

9/1 - Relapse: Client has relapsed so many times that she has given up at times. There were so many triggers but the main one, this time, was ANGER. Betsy stated, 'That's all I need as a reason to drink.'

9/2 - Group C: Betsy stated she was going to have a BBQ and to go swimming this weekend. She was polite and listened.

9/7 - Grp C Topic Defenses v. Boundaries: Betsy was engaged, but she began to cry when past hurts were discussed. She was emotional, and she asked to be excused. When she returned, she appeared to be doing better, and she finished group on a better note.

9/8 - Relapse: Betsy did not participate, and she said she was not feeling well. She said, 'have tried to stay sober with just will power, but it did not work because I did not have a plan to use when sober.'

9/12 – Betsy was on time. She participated. The HOH was struck by lightning. She really enjoys this group. She left to meet with CM.

9/14 - Group C topic 'Conflict Resolution skills for Healthy relationships': get in touch with feelings, be a good listener, practice assertive communication, seek solutions, know when it is not working.

Betsy was attentive, engaged, and she openly shared about struggles with anxiety and panic attacks. She was polite with appropriate interactions.

9/20 - PSYCH REPORT: Betsy never complained before, but she said that she does not like Haloperidol decanoates. She said, 'I don't like the way it makes me feel, and Trazodone gives me nightmares.' Begin Doxepin 10 mg. PRN- 4xday. Betsy denies that she still uses alcohol and refuses treatment.

10/17 - PSYCH REPORT: Betsy is misusing medications. She agreed to weekly restart of Fluphenazine decanoate.

10/26 - Group C topic: Different types of LOVE - How to respond to your spouse's wishes. Betsy had been absent for a while because she had just gotten a new kitten name 'Baby Blue.'

10/27- Betsy has been 'clean' and is allowed to visit family. She thinks about this trust as a tool to stay clean.

10/28 – She is doing well and then she began crying about her pet, Baby Blue.

11/1 – Betsy shared weekend experiences and how she dealt in a positive way. She is doing well.

11/2 - Betsy quiet, attentive, overwhelmed by excessive talking by peer. She excused herself and returned calmer.

11/3 – Betsy talked about her long history of heavy alcohol. She said she understands the connection between liver disease, alcohol and hepatitis.

11/4 – Betsy states, 'Mother takes all my money to be mean to me.' She avoids discussing her alcohol abuse as the reason. She expressed anger at the B&C, at the gay women who hit on her. She does not like it.

11/8 – Betsy is doing well. She had a good weekend. She enjoys coming to group and listening to others' opinions.

2012

1/24 - PSYCH REPORT – Betsy requests medications to be picked up every 2 weeks instead of weekly. She downplays amount of alcohol she consumes.

2/7 - SERVICE PLAN-Same

2/23 - PSYCH REPORT-Same

3/18 - PSYCH REPORT- Betsy says Naltrexone is helpful.

4/21 - PSYCH REPORT: Alcohol dependence in reported remission.

5/15 - PSYCH REPORT: Still drinks occasionally.

5/29 – Betsy is casually dressed, friendly, polite ,talkative, and feeling good.

6/12 - PSYCH REPORT: Neatly dressed, groomed, friendly, polite, talkative, good eye contact. She said she is 'eating, sleeping well, doing great, and she loves where she is living and hopes she can stay there.'

7/11 - PSYCH REPORT: Betsy's eating disorder is in full remission. She weighs 126 lbs. Her reported Alcohol dependence is full remission.

7/12 – She loves where she is living with Baby Blue. She is appreciative of Mom's and her CM's help with transportation.

7/17 – Betsy's new CM met at HOH with Betsy, her sister, and Betsy's Mom. Betsy likes HOH. She can swim, walk, watch TV, play games. Betsy was psychotic last week.

The crisis began when Betsy was unwilling to go to Compass. She walked away. 911 was called. The police followed her. It was rainy and hot. She spent 3 days totally disoriented. She was yelling and abusive. She showed Schizophrenic signs which have not been evident these last few years. The trigger for this incident was that the HOH would have to evict her because she had not eaten for 3 days. She had been panhandling in the park. She was getting 20 oz. beers and drinking steadily. She was abusive to residents. She was not sleeping, yelling, and keeping all from sleeping. She was very difficult in the ER when testing the alcohol limit legal. She had 1 beer at 9am. In the middle of 2nd St, the beer was forced out of her hand. The police were called. Betsy refused to go to Kino. She was experiencing terrible withdrawal. Another trigger was that John Sowersby, her CM, was leaving LFC without saying good-bye or any other closure. That hurt her. He had been with her 10 years. She felt abandoned with nobody to help. Finally, Betsy's childhood home is for sale. It is an intense time, very topsy turvy with moving boxes everywhere.

Betsy does not have any sense of resentment. Her mother couldn't bring her back to HOH, so she rented a hotel room. Her sister joined her. She has been evicted for hours. 'When she is not drinking, she is lovely.'

8/8 - PSYCH REPORT (Change of psychiatrist) – Betsy is a poor historian. She denies drinking, having mood swings, or depression. CM says she is an active drinker. She does not want her mother as part of her treatment. The physician does not want a Release of Information (ROI). Betsy does not want respite care when Mother is out of town for 1 week. According to Betsy, 'Mom needs therapy.' She likes where she is living and feels all her basic needs are met. She was alert, tracked conversation, and was wearing clean clothing. She stated she was 'doing well'.

Report of HOH caregiver: 'Betsy gets drunk often. She gets loud, slams doors, wakes everyone up in the house and does not sleep at night. Her behavior scares the household. She places dirty wash clothes that she wipes with on top of the bathroom counter. Often, the bathroom odor is foul. I have repeatedly observed her eating out of refrigerator containers. She dips her fingers in. It grosses all of us out, so that we cannot eat out of these open containers after she has touched them.'

9/10 - NURSE REPORT: She is neatly dressed, groomed, friendly, polite, and talkative. Her medications and injection are working well. She is eating and sleeping well. She is doing 'a lot of walking and swimming which she enjoys.'

9/18 - HOH CASE AIDE ASSESSMENT: Betsy exhibited polite mannerisms, good eye contact, good voice tone and volume. She was tracking the conversation as she answered each question. She was engaged. She exhibited good hygiene and is managing symptoms.

9/20 – Betsy is moving to her family's house temporarily. She will be back at HOH later. She feels safe and will spend time with family soon.

10/8 – Betsy does not like her mother being 'Bossy.' I 'become very anxious when I am around my mother.' She loves where she is living, and she is eating and sleeping well.

10/9 - SERVICE PLAN: Betsy reports being sober for One year.

10/12 – She is tired because her cat kept her up and then woke her up wanting to play. Betsy has been attending AA meetings. 'They are really helping.' She is not progressing toward improving her self-esteem, evidenced by body language (slouching), low volume of speech, lack of eye contact. She has been going to RP and SA Ed groups. She said she might be interested in classes. She visited HOH but did not go to group, 'I don't have much energy.' The service plan was mailed to her. She also received the certificate for MH Diversion graduation. She is now sleeping 8-10 hours per night. Before medications, she would wake up 2-3 times per night. She takes medications for ulcers too. She wants to switch medications to Naltrexone, which helped her with cravings, and Trazodone. She signed ROI for her mother. Her mother with her, and Betsy was quiet.

10/18 - Group C discussed Family Structures and how SA distorts them. That is motivation for sobriety. She was quiet but wrote responses to questions. Betsy benefits from group. It helps her to not want to relapse. 'I will practice skills I learned in my daily living'.

10/19- A Relapse Prevention talent show was put on to decrease boredom and to gain self-esteem. Betsy said she 'needs to be happy and to always do her best.'

10/26 - SA Ed: Left for bathroom and did not return.

11/6 - PSYCH REPORT: Betsy was disheveled with a decreased fund of knowledge. Her last intake of alcohol (ETOH) was 2 weeks ago.

11/12 - Betsy called in sick with a sinus headache. There was no RP group.

11/14 - A OK

11/27 - 'Great Thanksgiving with family and even saw sister from Nebraska.'

11/29 - B&C Assessment: Betsy does not want to move. She has better eye contact, and she is socializing.

12/11 – Betsy told the nurse that the medications and injection 'are very helpful. I had a great weekend spending time with family.'

2013

1/9 – Betsy had poor grooming. She said she 'ate a lot over the Holidays.'

1/13 - Rosa Chante Assisted Living Home. Betsy gave her reasons for relapsing. 'I don't know. I just started drinking.' She is 'taking her medications. Naltrexone helps. I like it here but I want to go home (HOH) when I get done.'

2/4 – The pharmacy made error by not filling her script. There was no problem with the injection. Betsy joked, 'You must've done good because I didn't scream.'

2/13 - PSYCH REPORT: She is now back at HOH. She commented about her stay at Rosa Chante's: 'I get along with everyone, and they cook really well there.'

2/19 - A OK

April, 2013 - She wants to switch to pill form not injection. She is beginning to have more anxiety, stress, and is not able to sleep. Her old behaviors are coming back: mood swings, high and low points, irritation, unpredictability. Recent changes have affected her. She is depressed that her family sold the family home that she grew up in. She is fearful that her parents will die. They are 80 years old this year. The family dog had to be put to sleep. At HOH others gossip about her and talk about her behind her back. She has trust issues. She feels comfortable talking with the nurse and will talk to her CM about 1:1 therapy. She is grateful for getting a medical bridge: 'I need my meds to maintain and to stay stable.'

5/2 – Betsy's mood is euthymic. Her affect is friendly. Her speech and thoughts are organized and relevant. She is clean and casually dressed.

5/13 - PSYCH REPORT: Betsy is not taking her medications properly. She missed her appointment because the doctor was not there. She was upset that doctor not there and that she was not told. She had a bad week. She drank 18 sodas and had mood changes. She has had an increase in hearing voices and is often agitated. That is affecting her living situation. She is not sleeping well, but she is eating OK.

JUNE 2013

6/3 - Crisis and safety plan: Betsy said, 'not taking meds would throw me off.' She wants to be sober until 12/13.

6/11 - A OK

6/18 – Betsy has been in Crisis Respite at Rosa Chante. She will not be able to see her cat for 1 more wk. CM said she had been actively drinking.

6/25 - A OK. Betsy worked out issues at HOH and is willing to stay.

7/1 - At CRC: 'They called the cops after I wouldn't come to the Thursday House Meeting.' Betsy's vitals, blood samples, and urine, came back normal. She said she feels 'bullied' at HOH. A petition was submitted to SAMHC to complete Persistently Acutely Disabled (PAD). It was submitted to MH Court. Betsy did not want a PAD, and she repeated continuously that she wanted to leave. She exhibited increased manic behavior: shouting , extremely impulsive, intrusive with staff, repeating questions over and over. She was also 'getting in staff's personal space.' She was very loud. Her CM talked with Betsy as she grew more and more anxious. She said, 'I just want to leave.' Her CM suggested that she take a nap to rest and pass the time. She would do that. She reported that she 'was out late with some friends and had 2 shots of alcohol.' Her mother called the cops. Betsy feels bullied by 2 residents. Betsy said that one woman who dispenses my meds is not a licensed nurse. Betsy does like living there, and it is really a beautiful house. CM offered Rosa's which has an open bed. Betsy wants to go there, but she wants to go back to HOH. She said, 'I like being there.' She is drinking Diet coke and trying to cut down on caffeine. Her mother reported she was not eating. When she came to the appointment, Betsy was laughing, talking about the weather, her allergies, and her housemates.

7/10 – Betsy was in a 'down' mood. She went to Compass last night and now has a nicotine patch on her left arm.

7/18 – She was at Compass for detox. She was discharged, and then she went to University Medical Center, and then to Rosa's. She was scared that she would be going to jail. CM said no. The Sheriff was coming to evaluate her. Betsy thanked her CM because 'You have instilled hope in me.'

7/22 – She is disheveled and is being moved to another residence.

8/1 - Mother petitioned her after she was out drinking with friends. She is now voluntary. She was discharged from UMC- South and is now at Rosa's.

8/5 – She had her injection. Her mood and affect were anxious.

8/13 - Betsy feels very lonely at Rosa's, 'like a caged animal. I cannot go out for walks. I feel locked up.' Her CM encouraged her to focus on her recovery and strengths, and to continue looking up. She will be able to return to the HOH at end of month. She feels increasing depression, as all others are physically disabled with Dementia, and they don't socialize much. She had a bad day. Her CM coming to visit makes it better. She wanted to go to the hospital, but now she said, 'Everything is OK. I am much better. My mother is coming to get me to take me out'.

8/19 – Betsy is unhappy at Rosa's assisted living setting. She is 'very sad', but gets to leave on 8/29. She often cries in bed and is only allowed 3 calls per day. She said they don't always give her the medications, saying 'You don't need these'. She admits to being in this situation because she had a relapse and is remorseful. She understands she has an alcohol problem. She said, 'I think it's about time at 51 to give it up.'

9/1 - Betsy said, 'I have been good and haven't been drinking.' She is back at HOH. 'TGIF'- Thank God it's Friday. Betsy keeps all her appointment cards.

9/5 – She is shivering with the cold in the office. At her mother's house, she had been drinking twice with some friends to celebrate their birthday. She said, 'I really want to stay at HOH.' Betsy was denied Level II alcohol inpatient treatment.

9/17 – Betsy is happy, energetic, smiling, and talking a lot. She took the dog for a walk this morning. We discussed the benefits of mild to moderate exercise.

9/18 – The dosage of Ativan was decreased for anxiety. Two relapses were reported.

9/27 – 'I have some cravings, but I am distracting myself with sweets, which I don't like since I am putting on weight.' Mentioned some other alternatives like Yoga in the Park. She said, 'I might try it'.

10/1 – Betsy is misusing her medications. Her mother helps with the counting. Someone broke into the medicine lock box. Bottles and pills were all spilled out. HOH is moving to a new location on Prince Rd. So her mother can bring her to appointments.

10/29 – Betsy is quiet, withdrawn, sullen. She said she 'just does not like needles.' She says she is not COT and asks why she has to have injections.

11/12 – HOH's recent move affected Baby Blue initially, but now all is fine. Betsy wants to switch to oral Fluphenazine.

11/25 - Lorazepam is being decreased to go back to Naltrexone. Betsy has been misusing it. She is taking it 1xday.

11/27 – Betsy wandered out of the house. She was found standing in middle of road, with traffic. She had a very bad day, but she was not trying to hurt herself. She feels lucky someone called the sheriff to pick her up. She is looking forward to holidays with her family. She said, 'they will be good, clean, sober festivities.' Now Hydroxyzine for anxiety.

12/8 - OP Admission LFC. She had alcohol 1-3 x last month. She began smoking cigarettes age 11. She has taken crack cocaine since age 28. She has not used it in 12 months. She requested a 'bubble pack' which was returned to the clinic in 3 months. Betsy overused her medications and was then hospitalized.

12/27- Betsy was discharged from the hospital with lithium and Lorazepam.

2014

1/3 – She feels much better talking with her sister in Nebraska. She overdosed 3 x's on her meds in 1 month.

1/9 - Staff met at Palo Verde Hospital for her SERVICE PLAN.

1/10-1/14 - Betsy was admitted to Palo Verde after going to TMC ER for overdosing on Lithium and Hydroxyzine. She is upset with her housemates at HOH. She needs to stabilize before being discharged and before returning. She is disorganized, psychotic, paranoid.

1/10 – Betsy said 'things have cooled down' back at HOH. She said she will 'hold on' until her next appointment.

1/16 – She was admitted to TMC. She was found on the floor with several empty bottles: Prolixin, Lithium, Trazadone (5 pills each) Her Lithium level was 2.5 which is considered toxic. She has high glucose and high potassium. She denies SI or HI.

1/17 - SAFETY PLAN: Triggers - 'When people are mean or bad to me.' She said she can prevent them by 'removing myself from the environment.' Her plan is to call her CM or take PRN.

1/18-1/21 – Betsy is in PHF. She is a DTS-Danger to Self. The reason is that as her mother was giving her medications, Betsy grabbed the bottle and took too many. She overdosed on Lithium. At the ART meeting her mother was concerned about her not eating in a healthy manner. Betsy was angry and in conflict with her mother. Her mother seems to have passive aggressive control issues with Betsy. Betsy has been compliant. She achieved goals: ' shower, take meds, go to group' Anxious.

1/23 – Betsy was discharged from Rosa's. She doesn't like it there because the clients are much older than she is. They acted strangely while walking around naked and defecating in bed. There is a pharmacy at Rosa's.

2/4 – Betsy repeated that she does not like being at Rosa's. The Ranch was offered, but she said: 'I've tried it before and do not like it.'

2/6 - Betsy is back at HOH.

2/11 – Betsy is back in the hospital. She had negative interactions with housemates and her mother.

2/13 - SAFETY PLAN: Stressors included negative interactions with House Mates; Claustrophobia; low self-esteem; stress; anxiety. Activities that help Betsy prevent relapses are: walks, smoking, phone calls, PRN, reading, her cat, music, meditation, TV, relaxing, taking a deep breath. How she wants to be treated in a crisis: respectful and with kindness.

2/15 – She made a contract with her mother for goals which included: Self-care; medication compliance; nutrition; sleep; exercise; hygiene; challenges and consequences. Spiritual goals included: Reading *The*

Four Agreements, attending church, journaling. Challenges facing Betsy include: Life Skills, Budgeting, cleaning, disposing of trash, doing laundry, phone calls, taking care of her cat, maintaining a support system.

> *2/16 — At Rosa Chante's: I am feeling very empty inside: depressed, dreary, gloomy, and nothingness. Doris, my roommate, is 78 years old. There is someone who is years old, but the remaining five clients are in their 70s and 80s and waiting on Hospice to die. It is very morbid. Most have Alzheimer's disease and Dementia. It is very sad, empty and depressing. The workers are mostly family and relatives. All of the doors are locked, under master lock and key. We are not allowed outside except for a small enclosed space in the backyard for smoking cigarettes. Rosa Chante is dedicated to Johnny's wife who passed away. It is locked down with three meals a day. There is coffee in the morning and snacks if you have your own. We have to go to bed directly after dinner and stay in our rooms until morning. Living here is taking all of my money, and I hate it here! I have been here before for Crisis Respite but never for this amount of time. I arrived on Friday, three weeks ago. So...., to cheer me up and constructively occupy my time, I*

decided to start journaling again, like I used to. Attitude of gratitude!

Thanks, Mom, for pen and paper. Yeah, Nannie! Luv ya!

So, with support from family, friends, La Frontera, my Case Manager, we are going to discharge and go to a transitional living situation before getting my own apartment to live independently on my own. I visited a friend in her fancy new one bedroom apartment with her dog, and it is very nice. I would like to get into an apartment myself. Fortunately, I have privileges to go out on passes. Mom, Rebecca, and I went to church. It was good to see my pastor and other familiar faces. I enjoyed church. Afterwards we went to Starbuck's and Carl's Jr for breakfast: Breakfast Biscuit, Omelet, Cheese and Sausage – Yum – Yum! Thanx, Mom!

It's now 4 pm. We eat supper very early. I hate it. All the other people in the house are old, grey, senile. It is very hurtful to me being here in lockdown with them. I am sorry, but I find it completely morose, morbid, sad and depressing. It is no fun. At least I can write and put my thoughts on paper. I have to eat at 4:30 pm. They served us chicken, BBQ sauce, green beans, buttered toast, and there was Kool-Aid with sugar which I did not

*drink. I have put on a lot of weight, extra lbs.
that I am afraid of. I am ready for this! !???
Up to about 140 lbs. YUCK! Am a fatty. Oh
no. How awful! I should go on a diet and get
back to 125 lbs. or less – which is where I was
before the binge eating started these past
holidays.*

*Speaking of the holidays, over Christmas,
New Years and my birthday, I spent a lot of
time in the Tucson Medical Center ER, Palo
Verde Psychiatric Unit, PHF on overdoses of
prescribed medications and alcohol. This was
when we were still at the HOH at Bel Air
Ranch Estates which was much nicer than
before. Unfortunately Mom and Rebecca
have closed the HOH, so..... there is no more.
I want out of here – I really do need out! But,
Mom won't let me live independently in an
apartment. She wants me to go to another
program – transitional living, which I don't
think I need. Well, ya know what?? I am
going to get out of this downer-down in the
dumps, sad – to let my mind, body and spirit
rest in Peace. Amen. And yes, I do take Jesus
Christ as my personal Savior.*

***2/17** – 5am woke up and went to smoke with
my roommate. It is dark still outside. I finally
got to sleep last night and had strange
dreams all night long. I am glad it is*

morning time: COFFEE! Yeah, luv it! It is true, so true. I need my morning caffeine, coffee and cigarettes. Yes: weight 133. 5 lbs. Lose weight. Coffee 5; Sodas 4; Cigarettes 20 – one pack. I am 15 lbs. over my desired weight. I will really watch out for what I eat. Spring is in the air. Time to shed off the winter's fat. I am going to have a beautiful day today. Good morning – watch the sunrise to the East. The stars are out of the sky – Lovely, Really Neat. I read the 'Daily Word – Silent Unity on Leadership'. A choice selection for President's Day. I will watch the sunrise. Good coffee. I luv u Tucson xxxOOO! Gonna have a good day – yeah!

7:35 am – Sunrise – Exquisite! All 'coffee'ed' out – Meds will be coming soon, and breakfast, but I usually don't eat – I don't do breakfast. Here the birds chirping, see the shining sun – Thank you, God! Thank you, God, for seeing me through my darkest hour, as I walk through the valley of the shadow of death, I shall fear no evil, for thou art with me – til the morning star rises to the east and sets to the west. AMEN! ALLELUIA! ALLELUIA! PRAISE THE LORD! A BRAND NEW DAY! I LUV Tucson. So the saying goes: You can take this two horse town; You can luv her; You can leave her. I luv my

Tucson!! True! I am not leaving Tucson-Pima County – It is home and I luv it!! xxxOOO EBM

8:10 am – I am just waiting until they get here: medications. No, they are not properly medicating me. I know what I take. It is not right. I am all messed up because of it, I know. I have been on psychiatric medication since I was a teenager which I had my first psychotic breakdown. It is true that they are not giving me what I need. I am very upset.

8:40 am – Medications: Fluphenazine, Lithium, Trihexyphenidyl, Omeprazole, Vitamin. Not much, but that is all they give me.

8:50 am – I don't usually do breakfast, but I think I will since it is not cereal and milk. I am here at Rosa Chante's as more of a Crisis Respite to detox. I have many deep-rooted, sad regrets about the HOH and losing it. I am very tearful, but Baby Blue is happy and all of my things, possessions are safe. I luv u, Baby Blue!! meow! meow! xxxOOO

9: 20 am – Scrambled eggs with tomato, onion and two sausage patties. Time for a smoke!

9: 40 am – Thinking about my son's father. True love forever. He left me the day of his mother's birthday. He had gotten our marriage annulled at Tucson City Court and left me for another woman. Downright broke my heart. I still luv him. xxxOOO. We separated on good terms, still best friends. Father of our Sweet Baby, 3/5/93 at Tucson Medical Center. My pride and joy. I luv u, son. Everything you say and do, who you are, real, is perfect – excellent in my eyes. I luv u unconditionally!! You are my everything. Son, I Luv You xxxOOO from your mother, Elizabeth, Betsy, 1/13/1962. I am Capricorn. I carry your photograph, picture wherever I go. I have always loved you. I always will. I Luv U xxOO

10 am – They are washing some of my clothes, laundry, wash and dry, which is kind of nice. This morning, I watched the news. Now, I am listening to KHYT 107. 5, classic rock 'n roll. Sunshiny day with a few high clouds. It is starting to warm up. It is almost lunchtime, but I am not hungry. I got to lose weight! Here is a beautiful poem from 'The Daily Word: This Deeper Love' by Donna Miesbach:

How silently the sun comes up,
With nary shout nor cry
And yet its sheer magnificence,

Lights up the broadening sky;
Oh may my Spirit shine like that!
May it rejoice and sing
Sharing thus this deeper love
With every living thing.

GOOD POEM

11am – My mother and Rebecca are
hopefully going to swing by later today
around 4pm for a hug and a visit, I hope.

11:40am - I ate lunch, toast, mustard,
sausage-chili, potato salad, a diet coke. I am
stuffed, feel fat, and I don't like this feeling.
YUCK! My clothes should be done soon. I took
an Ibuprofen and Hydroxyzine which should
help ease the pain, anxiety and stress. I want
to get out of here. I want to leave RC. It is hell
being locked in lockdown. I get phobic- a
phobia worse that paranoia. It is a real fear.
Claustrophobia, fear of being locked,
trapped, can't get out of small places. And
believe me, this is a small house. This
property probably isn't even an acre of land.
Yes, it is a fear, and I hate it here in lockdown.
I want to go. Real!!!
12:20pm - I really miss SO, I will pray for
you! My heart goes out to you. I know they

went to San Diego, and then Denver where her family is. But, I have had no contact. None whatsoever. I wonder how they are doing. My son will be 21 yrs old; I am so proud of our son. It must be a bitter cold winter in Chicago. I have seen the snow on TV. Can you believe it- 21 years old? I have not seen my son since he was 2 years old when his adopted family took him to New Jersey, South Africa, and now, Chicago. I wish he would come to Tucson to see his birth place and his real birth mother, me. But all I can do, son, is pray for you. God bless you and keep you. I love you, my son.

Yes, love you son! All I have are pictures, and letters, photographs. I would luv to share this journal with you sometime. It comes from my heart-love. From pictures, you are a fine young man, and I am sure-quite a gentleman. The photos of your real father SO. He is a good man and truly loves you, son. I see a lot of him in you! I care. Maybe we will meet again someday. I wish we could.

12:40pm I WEIGHED 139 LBS! What a bummer, downer. Ooooooh-fatty. I want to lose weight! It is true. Ya know?!I think of the family and close loved ones and friends very frequently through the day. I pray to God- God Bless!!It is very restrictive for me to be in lockdown. I want to get my own place, and apartment, someplace nice. But, mom wants me to go to a step-down, transitional living. I wish I could go today. This is just tearing me up inside out having to stay here against my own free will. It is true that I am not on court ordered treatment. I do not have to be here. I am voluntary, but my mother has control of my money, so I am stuck. My SSA, on the 1st of the month, goes to Project HOME, my representative payee. It sucks! I want my money! FUCK IT! I hate it and don't know what to do??? It is very frustrating and I just can't hack it.

1:35pm - I am hanging on to Mom, Rebecca, Dad, Sister, Aunt Alice and the rest of the family, our son, his Daddy for dear life. I need all the support I can get. I want out of here. I am crawling the walls. It makes my skin crawl. I am phobic. It is a very restless, disturbed feeing in here with the old people just waiting to die with Alzheimer's and Dementia. It is a feeling of nothingness, emptiness, sorrow, sadness, morbid unbearable depression. I can't use the telephone; I can't walk out the front door. It is terrible here. It is HELL, a living nightmare. There is nothing to do except smoke in the backyard, watch TV, and listen to the radio. Right now, I am sitting up in bed writing down on paper how I am feeling! I hate it. One of the men here actually died in here, and the rest of them look like they are going to. Very unsettling for me. It is hindering my recovery and disturbing the hell out of my mind. My nerves feel shredded. I am not even allowed to look out the window, let alone go out the front door for a walk. It is awful and I wish they would get me out of here!!! I mean it Mom, CM, please!??! I am begging you to let me go!? This place sucks. I can't even make phone calls. It hurts me pretty badly. I mean, it's like you have to even ask for a cup of water. I have to ask for everything. And then, the workers get mad.

2:20pm - Uh oh. I am eating candy, Reese's peanut butter cups-fat food. How awful! I am ruining my diet completely. I think I will not eat them. I will wait. Unfortunately, the temptation is there whereas before my 20 lb. weight gain, there was no desire at all. The craving will subside and pass; it will go away. I do not have to eat the Reese's. I won't.

3:45pm - Mom and Rebecca stopped by with Diet Coke, some meditations, and a hug, but we did not get to go anywhere. They couldn't stay. Mom has been working at school all day, and Rebecca is not doing well. They are tired.

So, here I am!! I am hoping that my CM and Mom can get me out of here. For real! I need out! Help me, God! Ease my pain-Spiritual, psychological, mental, body. My mind is racing- no sleep I hate it, it hurts!! Luv U Mom and Rebecca. God Bless you richly.

4:45pm – I already ate dinner: chicken, potato, carrots, tortilla and macaroni salad. I had my medications, Motrin, and Diet Coke. I love Mom and Rebecca so much. I miss them. I love spending time with them and with friends. I want OUT OF HERE!!I want to spend time with my family and loved ones, not at RC where old people go to die. I am at a higher level of functioning than that, and I know it. I can cook, clean, go shopping, do laundry, maintain hygiene, take care of an apartment and Baby Blue - meow, meow- and take care of myself responsibly. Not like being here where I can't do anything. I need to get out of here. I dread thinking that I have to spend another sleepless night here in this hell. Oh dear God, this feeling inside is not good; I hope and pray that tonight goes by quickly and that time will go by fast, so that it would be tomorrow already. And I hope and pray that I can leave tomorrow. God Bless my family, loved ones, friends and the people who pray for me. God Bless you and

*Keep You!! Have a good night Tucson! I luv
u! Night, night xx000*

2/18 *6:50am - Tuesday I weigh 134 lbs. and
drank 4 coffees, 6 sodas, 18 cigarettes and
iced tea. Well good morning! We watched the
sunrise. It is going to be a beautiful Tucson
sunshiny day! Blue skies and sunshine! Yeah!!
Good coffee and cigarettes. It is getting close
to 8am and time for taking medications. I
had a terrible night's sleep. I woke up in a lot
of pain! OUCH!! Today my CM is coming
over. Maybe, hopefully, she has found a
place for me. I will be leaving this hell hole -
RC. I hope and pray to be leaving today!
Yeah!!! Fingers crossed. Yesterday, I ate a
Reese's Butterfinger and a cookie. I think that
is why my weight went up. I skipped cereal
and milk for breakfast. Yuck! I am reading
'The Daily Word' on World Peace. The
reading is good.*

*8:15am - I need better medications or more
because this is not working. I feel like a
psychotic schizo with claustrophobia that has
not been properly medicated. Get me out of
this lockdown!! I have to try 'maintaining
stabilization' for my sanity or I will lose it.
Hopefully, I pray I won't. I am sound of mind.
Reading and writing keep me on track, as does
smoking in the backyard. I am just keeping*

my fingers crossed that the CM will come through for me today. If not, I am going to cry!

8:45am - I am going to take a shower this am before the CM comes over. I hope she brings good news for me! I HOPE! I have Pantene. It smells clean and really revitalizes my hair. I like it. It rinses really clean. I think I will shower around 10am. Sounds good! Hygiene!! Cleanliness is next to Godliness!! Shower-flower-power. Mom brought me clothes - new socks, underwear, tights - which is nice. Thank you, Mom, I luv u! Peace, love & Happiness. I will be out of here, but I just don't know when??!!

10:30 - Took a shower and now I'm all clean. Mom and my CM called.

11am-Almost lunch. I ate 2 bean tostadas. They put something in the food, it is poisoned; they do that in other places too, hospitals,, etc. Yuck! I do not want to eat anymore. I have gained weight! I Hate it!!! I am fat! I want to lose weight, and I can't here.

12:35pm - Good afternoon with my CM. She brought me a Starbucks coffee.

2/19 - *Woke up early to a beautiful sunrise. I drank 4 coffees and smoked 15 cigarettes. I weigh 135 lbs. I am really dieting starting now. Serious business! 'The Daily Word ' is*

*free. Mom stopped by for a hug. It was good
to see her. For lunch I ate 4 Taco Bell tacos. I
slept practically all morning, having been
woken up last night by roommate, and I could
not get back to sleep. I am tired. It is a grey
and hazy day. It's not too warm, and there's
no sun. I am thinking about leaving and
getting an apartment. There is a new
housemate, a younger female, who is very
nice. My CM says I have to go to transitional
housing before I can go to an apartment.
Meaning: no apartment, nothingness,
morbid, remorseful, sad, gloomy,
depressing, emptiness. RC- I hate it. I can't
sleep and have very disturbed and troubled
dreams. I can't diet and lose weight.
Lockdown is killing me!!! NO MORE.*

*2/21 - I can't go on living at RC. I turn it over
to God. I give it to the Lord. Let go and let
God. I don't want to read or write anymore.*

2/22 - SERVICE PLAN: Betsy said she wants to go
to Casa de Vida. She wants to be well. She said she
really feels her age and has daily physical pain.

2/23 – Betsy is now back at HOH.

*2/23 Relapse: I had all my medications, 2
cans of 8.1% alcohol Lager, Steele Reserve. I
walked down Grant from LFC to Fry's on
Alvernon. I bought a Black, mild cigar. If I
knew better, I would have taken all of my*

medications, drank those 2 cans of Lager and finished my life. If I knew that this feeling here at RC would be so bad. I did not do it. Sad regrets! I now wish that I had done it. So I called Mom from Customer Service, and she brought me to her home for the night. Then, early the next am, she dropped me off at RC. I have been suffering ever since. Lockdown is not a pretty picture. I wish I had done it while I was still on Grant Rd-took care of myself-too late.

At the pawn shop I sold my silver and turquoise pendant and 2 rings for $30 cash. I was sitting next to a very handsome man on a Fry's bench who reminded me of my ex. I could have took ....I would have went. Then, no more pain and suffering, sadness, hurt feelings- no more. It is too late. I hate RC. My CM is coming over soon. I want out of here!!! We are going to talk about housing and about where to go when I leave. My options are: CDV, New Directions, Primavera. I am thinking an apartment. I am just waiting, stuck at RC's. I do have an appointment on 2/20, so we will call about apartments. I hope it works out.

5pm Dinner: meatloaf, green beans, mashed potatoes, It was good. I had second helpings and a chocolate cherry. I am stuffed!! I have ruined my diet. Ugh! I will have to do better to lose weight.

5:45pm - I weigh 142 lbs. Yuck! I am a fatty! Fatso. O God help me!

2/24 - I want to be with my family. I have a family and I luv them. I am here for them because I luv them —my family. They are the only reason I am here. I am here for my family. I am waiting for my CM to call about housing either at CDV or New Directions. I am ready to go TODAY!

2/27 – Betsy was seen eating trash at Fry's Supermarket on Alvernon and getting a Bubble Pack from Walgreens.

2/28- TMC ER- Suicidal Ideation(SI). She was defecating in public and was dropped off at LFC. She sat on the sidewalk, waiting for her mother. Her Case Manager offered her a ride. Her speech was slurred.

3/1 - SERVICE PLAN: Go to the Thornydale Ranch to learn coping skills, improve ADLs, and to learn how to take meds correctly, to handle stress, cravings and anger. Met to discuss how Betsy's drinking problem will persist and will present as a crisis with nowhere to stay because of her drinking. She suggested attending groups to get prepared to go to residential treatment. Betsy agreed. Betsy is not making progress towards her goals, and was kicked out of the B&C for drinking while taking medications.

She became disoriented and confused. She is working towards change.

3/4 – Betsy was admitted to St. Joseph's Hospital, O'Reilly Care Center. She had overdosed on Lithium.

3/6- Betsy said that she overdosed because it 'helps me sleep' and that it was not SI. She agreed to go to The Ranch. She had an elevated blood count, a lethal dose of Lithium, a UTI, and she continues to feel anxious with her house mates at HOH. She said, it 'could be better; could be worse.' She will continue to use coping methods to deal with issues.

3/11 - ART meeting to coordinate care. Betsy agreed that she needed a higher level of care than living on her own. She agreed to go to The Ranch (Level II) to learn how to use meds correctly and how not to overdose on Lithium. She would learn how to take meds as prescribed, work on completing ADLs, and strengthen coping skills to avoid internalizing anger and stress.

3/13 – She is hoping to move from St. Joseph's Hospital to Casa Alegre. She is experiencing stress, anxiety, and depression. She was given another 24 hour notice and then rescinded it. Betsy was moved from RC to Oasis, a LFC facility. Betsy bombed out, bought ale, and was evicted. She went to O'Reilly-St. Jos Hospital Carondelet, Petition Unit. Papers were served for COT.

3/20- *At LFC with MOM. Court date Tuesday 9am-Casa Alegre*

3/14 – Betsy agreed that she is not ready to live on her own because she cannot take meds correctly. At Rosa's, they distribute medications, and she feels safe. New Directions may be the answer. Primavera Transitional Housing needs her to be working, and may not be a good fit. Betsy will stay with Level II. She wants to go to Casa de Vida or The Ranch. She also considered Oasis(supportive housing on Swan), filled out an application, and wrote a biography.

3/15 – Betsy went to Sonora for a psych evaluation.

3/17- Betsy will remain at Sonora.

3/19 – She wants to get out of St. Joseph's Hospital.

3/25 – Betsy was discharged from St. Joseph's to Casa Alegre. Her CM provided support in organizing daily activities and plan.

3/26 – Betsy is glad to be out of hospital and to be in Casa Alegre.

3/27- At the Sonora Behavioral Health Hospital. She requested SA Ed, Anger Management, RP, and AA.

3/25 - Pima County Superior Ct hearing: COT for 1 year reviewed with Betsy needing Level II.

3/28 – She is feeling nervous and anxious about the court hearing. She is using coping skills. Yoga is helpful.

3/31 – Betsy is at LFC after being D/C from St. Joseph's, Casa Alegre, and PHF.

4/3 – In Court: Betsy is nervous. She has been at Sonora and Casa Alegre. She has been exhibiting depression, anxiety, restlessness. She has been skipping meals, crying, and wanting to sleep. She feels others are attacking her. She is upset and is expressing feelings of SI. She is unhappy about not going back to HOH.

4/7 – The former house where HOH resided is now for rent.

4/16 – Betsy has been discharged from Casa Alegre to The Ranch. She wants to stop Lithium and Hydroxyzine because of the side effects: dry mouth, stomach upset, nausea.

PSYCH REPORT: Betsy is casually and neatly dressed. She is pleasant, cooperative, and has improved in all areas.

> *4/16 TR –My new doctor has my meds all messed up! Bummer!!!!? I am sorry I haven't been writing too much. It has been difficult for me to put pen to paper. I can't quite put down what's on my mind and how I am feeling into words.*
>
> *4/17 Circle K run - I snuck 2 little shots, 'airplane shooters' of dark Bacardi Gold rum.' So you know, and how about that?! I called Mom, Rebecca, and my sister (could not get thru) a bummer, because I really wanted to talk with her and my CM .*

4/18 – She thinks the Ranch is better this time than the previous 2 times. She wants to have a Judicial Review and discuss finances at the next ART meeting.

4/23 - Betsy likes helping take care of animals during Barn group. She doesn't like the stigma of being on COT.

4/27 – Betsy's goal is to love herself and her family. Her mother visited. Betsy is doing well. She is monitored every 15 minutes. She did not do chores or go to barn grp.

4/28 – Betsy wants to engage in therapy to learn coping skills, improve ADLs, and learn how to take meds correctly. She really likes the Ranch. Her mother came to visit. Betsy said it was really nice to see her. They had a good visit. 'I wasn't welcome in their home a lot if I was drinking alcohol and using drugs. I felt sadness and shame. I want my parents to be proud of me, and I don't think they are.' She was tearful with unresolved grief over the loss of her son and her son's father, 'the love of my life.' Betsy is stuck in the stages of anger and depression. She has had many losses: son, man, other friendships, family, hope, self-respect, self-esteem, trust. 'I can't feel losses because I am over medicated which numbs my feelings so much.' It was suggested that she write in her journal. Betsy agreed.

'I need to watch what I eat. I am now 133, and I want to lose 10 lbs. I like myself better at 125. I got down to 103 once because I was not eating at all. I don't want to do that again. She watches her weight as a way of feeling in control of her life. She reported feeling hungry at the end of the session, and she wanted to eat lunch.

Betsy's affect was: blunted, sad, anxious. She always thanked her CM for coming to the session. Betsy admits to having urges and cravings. She wants a Smokers Anonymous Group set up to help her and others quit smoking. She did not complete ADLs and hygiene.

4/29 – Betsy is drinking Ensure to supplement less food intake. She drinks 7 sodas daily. She is very social with peers. She interacts positively and wants to attend the NA group. She went but it was cancelled. She always takes PRN: 2 Benadryl, 2 Tylenol, and Milk of Magnesia. She said she takes these medications because of clogged sinuses from allergies, aches and pains, age, and they help her sleep. Betsy wants off COT there is a reason to stay on COT. Her behaviors of overdose consistent with SI; thus she needs inpatient facilities. She also abuses alcohol and is noncompliant with meds.

4/30 – Betsy has been giving away her cigarettes. It was her third time being reminded not to. She does not always do chores. She wants to start daily walks in the AM and the PM.

5/1 – She wants a soda every hour, but staff reminds her that it is not good for her. The CM reports that Betsy's concerns included not being able to get off COT. The team wants to see progress in treatment first. She showed her CM the animals and the barn. She said how much she enjoyed working with the animals. She talked about her pony, Patches. Her CM asked her how she spends her days and if she feels she is benefiting from TR. Betsy is nervous about the ART meeting. She was reassured that her mother will be here.

5/2 – Betsy was in a serious and unapproachable mood. She did not eat dinner, but she ate 2 candy bars for snacks. ART Meeting we discussed her goals: remaining sober, managing her moods, being well and what that meant to her, eating habits. She wants a place that accepts cats. She also wants a patch to help stop smoking. She said that she is OK with staying on COT, and she wants to go to Oasis if it will accept her.

> *5/2 Staff is really strict here: Coffee, cigs, snacks, meds, grps, barn, meals,*
> *Barn Group. I fed horses: 2 male, 2 female, 3 donkeys, 2 pigs, 1 goat. I love the animals, but they are very unkempt, dirty, neglected. Most of them are old- not for riding, they have fly masks over their eyes to keep the flies off them, but it doesn't work; the flies are terrible! Nobody ever takes them out to groom them- nothing but am and pm feeding. I feel for the animals. It is sad to see such suffering. I have asked staff and Holly, the therapist, about it but they won't do anything about it. How sad! It is almost dinner 5pm. I*

am not going to eat. I am going to lose weight. I can only weigh once per week on Sunday. I like myself better when I am running about 125 lbs. or less. So I am on a diet!! Real. Medications at 7am and 7pm. Snacks at 8:15pm. Reading 'The Daily Word' really hit home! I luv my family. I don't want to lose them. May they be long lived. God bless Mom and Dad, Rebecca, Sister, my son and everyone else in the family. I maintain a hopeful, positive attitude! I Luv !!xxxooo

5/2 - 6:15pm watching sunset to the West. We are really out in the desert. 7pm Group Meetings. Medications, snack. End of another day. I luv U, Tucson. Until tomorrow xxooo Goodnight.

5/3 - Betsy has been compliant with all expectations. She wanted 2 diphenhydramine pills, but she was told that they can damage her liver. She already has liver disease.

5/3 7:30am - JUST WOKE UP Good morning! BEAUTFIUL, sunshiny day. Yeah!!I woke up in pain —body aches-but hopefully it will go away. Staff is cooking breakfast, but I won't eat. I want to lose weight. I want to ask if they will let me weigh myself, but I don't think they will let me. Blood pressure is also taken on Sunday. Mom will be visiting tomorrow, which will be nice. God bless you, Mom! Luv U! We have an outing, movie, bowling, something like that, Walmart. So, I am hopefully going to have a good day!

9am- *I ended up eating breakfast: 2 French toast, 2 sausages, hash Browns with syrup and OJ. Yum! I am glad that I ate. I also drank 2 cups of coffee. I missed Barn group. I am tired and in pain. I think I will lay down for a while . First, I went to morning group, drank 1 12 oz. can caffeinated Diet coke, smoked and then lay down. I talked to Mom and had a good phone call! I am looking forward to seeing her at noon.*

Lunch was meat, cheese, tomatoes, mayo on white bread and punch. I want to weigh myself. I am afraid to ask because staff will probably say no. I have to wait until Sunday. It is such a bright, sunshiny Saturday. It reminds me of the good old days by Tanque Verde and Sabino Canyon and by Grant and Craycroft with my drinks, drinkin' buddies and a lot of good spirits. I luv u! xxoo Mt. Lemmon – Santa Catalinas- my favorite mountains. I really, really miss '9020'. Desertedge, very, very much! I luv that house!! It is empty inside-we don't get to go back; boo hoo.

They have my medications so messed up; they really do. The side effects are terrible. I feel like shit all of the time. It's not good. This feeling I have is awful. I can't get well here. I want to go home to Eagle Feather, but I can't. Bummer!! I am very sad and depressed. I fell all beat up. I didn't have any caffeine, hardly any. This environment is tearing me up. The showers suck. They are dirty. I want to be with my family and friends on the NE side of town. All of my things are there. I want to go. This COT is awful! I hate it!! Flippin' you the bird. FUCK OFF! Let me live my life instead of this prison, being used and abused. I have been enslaved for no damn reason. Hell with it. My D/C date is June 16, and I will go away or else!! I am just laying down in bed trying to pass the time of day which it seems to me is going by very slowly. Attitude: I will maintain a hopeful and positive attitude! The light is bright; the sun is fun; the skies are blue; the grass is green, and I luv u. I LOVE YOU ELIZABETH, UNCONDITIONALLY.

Just loaned someone $5.00 to be paid back next week. I finished barn group. It was good to be feeding the animals .

4pm – Medications and Dinner: spaghetti, meatballs, garlic bread. Yuck, I ate too much. I feel fat and ugly. I want to lose weight. They are going to Walmart; I am not going. I am stuffed. I think I will smoke and lay down. WOW! I luv u Tucson. Ya know: Being here in the desert at TR reminds me of Apache Red Eagle, 'Patches' 14.2' hands high, registered Red Roan Appaloosa Quarter Horse. We showed in the 4-H and the Pony Club horse shows. I love Patches, my little show pony!! I have a terrible headache right now. PAIN has been going on for a while now. Nothing seems to remedy my pain. I want alcohol and sleep. I do not feel good. I have a steady, aching, sharp pain, almost feels like a burning sensation. I really do not like this feeling. I guess you could say I have tended to lose my smile! I don't have that good, good feeling anymore. Maybe it is too much of the medications, or maybe the wrong kind. I just don't know what to do to get well- to be happier- to be feeling better????!!!!I am going to eat KitKat potato chips, cheese crackers, and snacks. I really don't want to, maybe I won't. But Yes, I do want to lose weight. Dinner was disgusting! I just sold a pack of smokes: not good, a big No-No. I am signing off for the night and pray for a better day tomorrow. Luv U! Peace, luv, happiness!

5/4 - Betsy's mom brought lunch, ice cream and cake for the birthday of one of the residents.

Sunday 5/4 - *7:30 awoke, Good Morning! 132 lbs. meds, breakfast (mostly Ensure) but sesame seed bagel with cream cheese, scrambled eggs and ham; another beautiful sunshiny am her at TR. Mom is coming to visit. YEAH! I can't wait to see her! Hi Ho! xx00 Luv Ya! 1pm —Had an excellent visit with Mom and my friend. We had McDonalds, and we called my sister in Nebraska. We had photos too! I want copies of them. After they left, I feel empty inside. I am sad and depressed. But, I can celebrate our special moment together. And, with a positive attitude, hope we will be in touch with each other, soon! I LUV U!xx00 I feel like crying when I remember the hugs and kisses are over. I was watching them drive away through the gate in the Toyota Prius Hybrid with license plates marked THE ONE! I love you, Mom & B. I wish I could have gone!! I miss you!!I took my noon meds. It is very quiet now. Writing in my room . It is dark & the AC is cold. I think after I go smoke, I will lie down & take a nap for a while & listen to the radio. Okay!!! 2:30pm I went to pick flowers for Mother's Day! I luv you son I luv Mom! I signed Dad's 81 birthday card. Long live Mom & Dad! Yeah!! Truthfully I hope, real, that they outlive me!!!Yes!! Dinner:*

juice, diet coke decaf, Ensure. You know, I called my friend on the phone. She and my friend are not on speaking terms. I love my Heart sisters. I called Mom. My D/C date is 6/16. I got here 4/16. Mom wants me to stay longer, 6 months to a year. Mom and I were speaking of keeping up a good support system. After Mom, Dad and Rebecca pass away, I will start crying. I don't want them to go.

Mon 5/5 - What a beautiful morning! I walked out, and the sun is shining. The birds are chirping, and it is a brand new day. The horses look hungry! We feed them at 8:30. I am still having a problem about caffeine. One 6oz cup is not enough. Then, my medications on top of it. I feel slow, tired, lethargic, and groggy! Not a good feeling-lack of energy! Had an Ensure and apple juice. I smoked a few cigarettes, made my bed, got dressed, and read 'The Daily Word.' I am thinking about home: Mom, Dad, Rebecca. It was really good seeing my friend. Her birthday is 1/15. I will hopefully have a good day!! I just completed Barn Group. I am feeding and watering. I luv the 5 horses, 3 donkeys, 2 pigs, and 1 goat. I have to wait for my second coffee. I am still very groggy, YUCK! Group is in *another building, Mt. Rose. What I do like about TR is the cold AC. I like being able to walk out in the back patio to smoke and to see the animals. I luv them! xxoo I wish I could do more for them. We'll see.*

Letter to our son: 3.5.93

I luv u, son! xxoo I think of you all of the time. I want to hold you hug you. I tell you how much I luv U. xxxoooo I hope you understand and accept my feelings and forgive me for my problems. I luv u unconditionally, son. True luv forever. I haven't seen you since you were 2 years old! I miss you. Maybe someday, we could see each other, talk on the phone, sending pictures, money for you, and letters in the mail. When do you think you, maybe, perhaps, at your convenience, will come to Tucson? I would love to see you! They are going to give me my many medications. I want to get back on Lorazepam, Ativan. I miss home- the Northeast side. I really, really want to go! I really don't feel like writing anymore, so I won't. My therapist encouraged me to write, especially for you. I hope you will read these. For me,

it is hard to find the words that would describe my feelings of luv that I feel for you, our son. I luv u unconditionally, my son. You will always be my Sweet Baby, son of SO, and yes, son, I am still your mother Elizabeth!!! I will probably not write like I used to, I am sorry. EBM

Letter to William S. Masland, Dad, on May 17, 2014

Dear Dad,

There are so many things I have wanted to share with you and talk about and spend time with you. I do love you, Father, and I am hoping that you can find kindness in the pit of your heart to forgive me! I care!! I suppose I feel like I was not the daughter, you had wanted me to be. I apologize. I have changed my ways, Dad. I am in recovery, therapy, and a healing program here at TR. I understand I have problems, and I am working on them. Dad, I guess just basically I never really felt that I was good enough for the family. My best wasn't good enough. I am sorry! I cry a lot. I am very sad and depressed. And, Dad, I want to really thank you, with a real

attitude of gratitude for all that you have done for me since I came into this world on January 13, 1962. I love you, Dad. HUGS!

May 5-Cinco de Mayo I got my 12 oz. can of Diet coke, caffeine, my next one will be two hours later. It is just about time to go to group. All for good! Good group! Next one is SMART group-self-management and recovery therapy treatment. It is getting hot outside! I miss Eagle Feather and swimming!! Luv u Tucson! Holly-Equine therapist will meet me 1:1 tomorrow. For lunch I had Chocolate Nutritional Plus Milkshake. I am serious about getting down to 125lbs or less. I tried to phone Mom and Rebecca. There was no answer after 3 phone calls. Just a recording. I will try them later. I Luv them! Xxxooo. This daily structure gets pretty boring; the same thing over and over. No fun. Ah well, maybe it's for the best. Happy Cinco de Mayo! Dinner: chicken strips, macaroni, cheese, mixed vegetables, I hate to say it, but I am in pain.

5/5 - She made progress in all areas, and it is important to maintain hope and a positive attitude.

5/6 - 1:1 Therapy: She has been journaling a lot. She has been processing feelings of sadness, guilt, and grief about losing her son. She has unresolved grief and loss about her relationship with her father. 'I'm dwelling in regret about the past. I have so much regret about my relapses. I started drinking with my older sister and friends when I was 8 or 9 years old. I was too young. Then I found out about boys when I was too young. My father does not talk to me. He is too emotionally sensitive. He has his own issues, and it's too hard for him to talk to me. I love him so much and want to talk to him. I haven't talked to him in a year. I have so much I would like to say to both of them, but I can't find the words.' She will decide later whether to send them letters, and she would bring them to the next therapy session.

She discussed options for post TR, such as 'Oasis House.' But the last time she was there, she said, 'I got too happy and drank alcohol. I took too many medications. So I relapsed. They said I could not go back there.' Her mood was sad, anxious, and guilty. She admitted to cravings and urges to use substances and drink.

She asked repeatedly for soda, and was refused it. 'I know why you're doing this. It's just to be mean to me and piss me off.' She talked over others and rude to peers and staff. In the van for the AA meeting, she apologized to staff for 'making such a big deal out of sodas and cigarettes. That's not what's important; my recovery is.' CM reported that the doctor does not want her to switch her medications because of the interaction with other medications. The doctor will bring it up again. Betsy is sleeping well, but she has nightmares. She still likes the barn group best. The CM talked about an extension to go into effect after her first discharge date. Betsy understood and said she would think about it.

> *5/6 - Good morning, good morning, woke up, made my bed, smoked, had coffee, got dressed for the day. Going to have a good day. Last night, I had a strange dream about my son when he was a newborn. In the dream I was carrying him in my arms, very peaceful and restful. Dad was in my dream also. He was sitting in a chair with his hands folded in his lap. He didn't say anything. He just looked at me. I think I dreamed this because of what Holly and I talked about in our session - to write both my son and Dad a letter, grieving them through the stages of Grief: denial/shock, anger, bargaining, depression, acceptance.*
>
> *We have a gardening group. Tonight we get to go to a 12 Step meeting - NA/AA Recovery! My CM called me from LFC. We transplanted plants into larger pots. I love life! Live and*

let live!! I talked to Mom, and she was busy. Hopefully, we can talk later today. I had 'milkshake', diet coke, and juice for lunch. Barn group is my favorite. I spoke to Holly about getting to weigh myself more than once a week. We talked. I obsess with my weight. It is something I can control. I gain a sense of self-worth about how much I weigh. I accept myself now- being healthy, even though I have put on a few pounds.

5/7 - I haven't been writing today. I am sorry. It has been breezy, very windy outside, in the low 70 degrees. It is very cool for this time of year. We went to Circle K. I bought a 44 oz. drink and candy bars. I have sabotaged my diet. Oh no!! I have to get back on track! I want to call Mom. Hopefully I will get a good night's sleep. I wake up in the morning and feel pain-body aches- headaches. I love you, Mom, Dad, Rebecca, family and dear loved ones, friends! May God Bless you richly! xx000 I luv u Goodnight! I am not going to write anymore for a while. We did Barn Group-fed and watered. It is very windy outside- a lot of dirt and dust in the air. Night, night, I luv u Tucson! God Bless! I pray for a better day tomorrow. I tried to call Mom and Rebecca but a recording. Bummer, I am very empty and sad inside. I want to go home. I am homesick. I want the comforts of home.

5/7 – Betsy walked the 'compound'.

5/8 – So-so compliance today.

5/9 - Because of the heat, staff kept cancelling the barn group. Betsy was disappointed, but she still gets points. She had a protein shake instead of lunch. She asked when the animal group would start up again. She was reassured that they would start up again as soon as the new animal care staff came. She went on the library trip. She is making progress in all ways.

5/10 – She has made progress in all ways.

5/11 - Affirmation: 'I love you Elizabeth unconditionally.' Her goal is 'to go on the Saturday outing.'

The bowling alley sold her beer. She took it outside. The employees would have called the police if she had not been part of LFC, as it is illegal to take alcohol outside. There was an empty beer can in bathroom. She had a styrofoam cup of "soda." When we tried to get it, she held on it. She would not let it go, saying 'This is mine. You can't have it.' Staff said they had to look to be sure it was soda. 'Of course it is soda, what else would it be?' She denied buying beer and said the bowling alley staff lied.

After others were dropped at TR, staff were supposed to take her to CDV for a breathalyzer test. She was not in the bowling alley, so staff looked at a near-by store. So staff took Betsy to CDV directly while others stayed in the van. She blew .008. She was to go to NW Hospital for medical clearance. Betsy got very angry, raising her voice at staff, saying 'They are lying.' Then she said she bought the beer for someone else, despite being told she was seen going into the bathroom with the beer. Betsy said she did not want to talk about it anymore. She did not admit to drinking beer until she was in the van. She said, 'You are inconveniencing me over one lousy beer.' We ignored her and let her ramble. She was still very upset. 'The staff are trying to punish me. I know what they are going to do, they are very barbaric. You are going to just drop me off & leave me-why?' She was very afraid of being D/C. So she was reassured that it is just a formality. She was still safe and would remain with staff while in the ER. She will not be able to go on outings for a long time because staff does not trust her.

She was compliant in every other way. "I can't wait for my mother to get here." Her mother arrived with soda and peanut butter crackers (Too many, so her mother was given 6 packs back. Betsy did not seem upset. She missed group because she called her mother even when reminded to get off.

5/11 Mother's Day-

Yeah! Wow. I haven't written for a few days now. Gee, yesterday, we went on our outing to Golden Pin Bowling Alleys on Miracle Mile. Well, I had some Diet Pepsi, and then I went outside to smoke. I walked over to the store and bought a lager and drank it in the bathroom. I bought some trinkets from the gumball machine. Then I bought a Budweiser Clamoto from the concessions stand and drank it in the bathroom.

Busted!! The bowling alley staff told our staff I was drinking in the bathroom so I ran away. I picked up one more lager, and then crossed Miracle Mile. Staff came running after me, so I went back. They brought me to CDV for a breathalyzer test and I blew .08, so the they took me to NW Hospital ER to get medically cleared. I drank that lager in the hospital bathroom. They took my clothes, handbag, vitals, urine, and drew blood. So, anyhow, after waiting 3.5 hours in the hospital bed, they cleared me. WOW! And let me go. I made it back to TR. I took my meds, ate dinner, and went to bed. What a day!

5/12 - I called Mom and Rebecca. Mom was going off at me, thinking I wanted to commit suicide. Well I don't. She always blows things out of proportion. She exaggerates. Well, it is a beautiful sunshiny Sunday. Yesterday is gone, and tomorrow isn't here yet. All I have is today-right here, right now. A brand new start! I really don't want to hear from Mom and Rebecca about the drinking —I really don't. I weigh 135 lbs. I have put on weight. Ah well, I will have to get back on my diet. I had a milkshake earlier for breakfast-it was good. God bless.

I am going to have a good day today, I hope. I am not going to go on and on about the Relapse. I could say 'I'm sorry' but that would be a lie. I enjoyed every taste of the 2 lagers and 1 Clamato. And that's that. I am not proud, but it was good! I walked over to Mt. Rose and traded cigarettes for coffee. Not good!!! I am running low on Pall Malls! I only have 4 packs left. Oh no! I don't want to run out, Ya know. I spent a lot of money yesterday- too much uh oh.

Mom and Rebecca came by to visit me today. Happy Mother's Day! We had subway sandwiches and talked. I got to hear from my sister in NE and from Uncle George in ME. Aunt Alice isn't doing too well.

I just hope I can get out of here soon. That is what I am thinking. 'I want to get away; I want to fly away. Yeah, yeah, yeah. I luv u, Son. Xxxooo. You are gorgeous, a very handsome man; quite a gentleman! I love the new photos. Son, you will always be my Sweet Baby and also my pride and Joy. I luv u!'

You know, I should be grateful with a real positive attitude of gratitude for the blessings I receive. There is so much out there to be thankful for that has come to me so far in my life time! It is really quite overwhelming!! I really want to stop pushing about the medications getting straightened out-they are all messed up ...The Diet Coke, coffee, Pall Malls, candy, crackers, eating, $, and alcohol. Just take TIME OUT- deep breath and 'Let go and let God'! I can't. He can, 'Please GOD HELP ME! Amen. I tried to call home and got a recording-Bummer. I am homesick, and I want the comforts of home and family! I miss Eagle Feather terribly!! I cry!! I will miss the swimming- Desertsedge I luv 9020!! It will never be the same- I am without! Empty, sad inside-missing Eagle Feather, Desertsedge-homesick, crying, I luv u 9020!

Dinner: cheeseburgers, French Fries, beans, pink lemonade. I have been eating too much and I know it!! I want to lose weight. I weighed 135 lbs., and I want to drop 10 lbs. if I can. I hate to admit it, but I have been craving alcohol. I can't help this feeling, both physical and psychological. It happens to me frequently even after yesterday, after 3 cans of lager- that was just a tease.

Thank God TR took me back. I am very grateful to be here. But, I am longing for home, homesick, wanting to go there, missing Eagle Feather, and Dad's birthday party. That I can't even go to. What next?? I just talked to Mom. God Bless you Mom. The greatest, most, bestest Mom in the world! I luv u! No negativity, just pure, sheer Serenity with a real positive attitude of gratitude! Change happens. It is going to be alright. It will get better. Changes are for the good.

5/12 - CRISIS and SAFETY PLAN: Betsy experienced daily sadness, depression, low self-esteem, cravings and anxiety. It was suggested to Betsy to use her strengths: friendliness, compassion, helpfulness, loyalty, ability with animals, caring to help her. She wanted to be D/C: 'Living independently in her own apartment, budgeting her own $, getting her own groceries, riding the Sun Tran, and staying clean and sober.' Triggers included: cravings and being isolated. Suggested prevention of relapses: participate in groups and take walks. When in crisis she wants to be treated professionally and respectfully. 'I do not want to feel pushed aside.'

5/12 - What a day! My CM drove over to update my Service Plan and to extend my

*stay here for an additional 60 days from 6/
16. The plan is for my stay to be 6 months. I
hate to say it, but the cravings are really bad.
I want to go! I won't be writing too much for
a while. I need some timeout. I luv u
Tucson,xxxooo I am homesick.*

5/13 – Betsy appeared to be under the influence of
alcohol. She smelled, and she visibly appeared to be.
She was disoriented, behaving in a bizarre manner.
Her eyes were watery, and she had difficulty
articulating and concentrating on conversation
topics. She went to NW Hospital for medical
clearance when the others returned from an outing.
Betsy kissed a male peer on the lips and hugged him.
'Oh, I am sorry. I probably messed up.' She was
separated for this inappropriate behavior. She sold
cigarettes to a peer. Staff confronted her, she said,
'OK, I'm sorry, I'll never do it again. Cross my heart
and hope to die.' She went to an NA meeting.

5/14 - 1:1 Therapy: 'I just feel so bad about what
happened at the bowling alley. I just bought 2 beers
and drank them because I was so happy.' She
processed feelings of guilt, sadness and shame. 'I
learned that cravings and triggers can be so strong.
Relapse can happen very quickly. That area of town
and the alley are familiar to me. I just wanted to
drink.' We developed a safety plan. She agreed to talk
with staff or peers if she is having strong urges or
feels triggered. She stayed away from the alley for

the time being. Betsy is motivated to change, but she still contemplates using.

I am fearful of losing my parents, and she hopes to die before them, as she depends on them financially and emotionally. She was tearful as she processed fear and sadness. 'I want to be close to my Mom and Dad. I'm scared of losing them before they can ever be proud of me. I am grateful to be able to stay at TR after relapsing, grateful, sad, but hopeful.' Betsy will apply for an extension at the TR. She was prompted to eat at least one meal, and she said she would eat dinner.

5/15 – Betsy is fine. She listened to her favorite radio stations during the ride, but she became increasingly anxious as she approached the office, even more so when Mom was not there. She demanded to call her mother, but needed to fill out paperwork; then her mother walked in. She was calmer. She was very happy to see her Mom. She was cooperative and compliant. She smoked, and she said, 'I will stop selling cigarettes and will tell staff each time they ask me for one'. She stayed a whole hour at an AA group in the evening.

5/16 – Betsy kept berating staff for a soda despite being reminded that a limit had been agreed upon. She was instantly angered, poor emotional regulation, yelling and cursing, unable to be redirected. Agitated and confrontational all day, she was verbally aggressive: 'You guys treat us like a child. What's it to you that I have a soda? Do you get a power trip from it, or something? Well, fuck you! Why don't you get an education, you ignorant shit?' She was talking over staff and attempting to manipulate the situation to her advantage. She was reminded that staff was here to support everyone, to implement rules and to implement decisions made by the team. Betsy was highly unpleasant and inappropriate during the interaction. She called her CM about wanting to leave and live independently. Her team does not feel it is a safe to move. Betsy feels her current medications make her tired and give her nightmares.

> *5/17- '33, Dad's 81st birthday, and I am getting him a shirt and a card. I love Mom, Dad, and Rebecca so much. I don't want to lose them! They are getting old. It would be so devastating to me if they died. It would just tear me up inside. I am like thinking God will make my Judgment day come first, so that I wouldn't have to suffer the grieving, mourning, sadness and depression I would go through if they died. I am still so dependent on family, especially Mom, Aug 1, 1934. It scares me to think about it. I love the family.*

5/18 - She took a walk after taking her Ensure. She had a confrontation with a peer, possibly about cigarettes. 'I need to get out of here and take a walk'. She did not want to go on the movie outing. Her mother came and brought food. When she left, Betsy worried that her mom had filed a COT petition. She made many calls.

She was reminded that due to the past incident, she could not go on the store outing. She was not in a happy mood and was anxious and angry at staff. She had called the LFC Crisis Line, 'My life had been threatened, and I don't feel safe at TR. My rights are being violated by the TR staff. I'm being kept against my will. This isn't a Crisis, and I'm not hurtful to myself or others. The LFC doctor is not prescribing me the right meds.' Betsy thanked the Crisis Line for listening. Her concerns would be given to the CM. When asked, she said she did not feel that way any longer and would talk to her CM in the morning. The problem concerned her family and 'did not involve anyone here.' They had misunderstood her, and 'I never said anything of the sort. It's my family I am concerned about because Mom brought Living Will paperwork.'

She became verbally abusive: 'FUCK YOU' when I needed to verify the name of the medication before giving it to her. She said 'You are uneducated.' Then she was later pleasant, agreeable and polite to staff. She did chores and showered.

5/19 - A good day

5/20 – Betsy had lab work done, and she appears to be doing well. 'The AA meeting was very helpful therapeutically.'

5/21 – It was too late for the barn group.

5/23 - Betsy stated 'I am not doing well.' She was upset when denied a soda 'You treat me like a child here.' She called Mom , and then she called 911 on behalf of a female peer, an unspecified emergency. The Sheriff arrived to speak with the peer, and Betsy was told not to call again but to speak to staff instead. She was redirected from drinking soda in her room. Betsy's response, 'Mind your own business. Geez, it's just a soda. I don't see why you have to bother me all the time. Well, whatever, I think it's stupid.'

She asked for soda at dinner and was denied, 'This is so stupid.' At the NA meeting she bought 2 sodas; though she had been told the cut-off was 5 pm. She said, 'Mind your own damn business, geez!' After the meeting, she bought another one. When asked why, she angrily replied 'Why do you care, it's not your business. It's no big deal; it is your problem.' Staff responded that the big deal was dishonesty, sneakiness, and trying to break rules she understood and had been reminded of twice that afternoon. Staff asked for the soda. Betsy responded, 'No way man. Get your own soda.' Later at TR in response to a request to give up her the sodas, she said, 'My roommate, whatever her name is, is sleeping, and

I'm changing clothes, don't come in.' When she came out, she said, 'I don't have them.' When asked again, she said, 'I told you that I don't have them. I left them there.' Staff said they did not believe her. She walked away huffing and cursing them under her breath. She tried to split the staff by asking one staff member and then another when told "no" by the first staff member. She also asked a peer in the other house for coffee. When asked about it, she said, 'I didn't ask him for anything.' She asked for Ensure at dinner, and she was told "no," and so she asked other staff for Ensure. She left angry, cursing staff, saying 'Go Fuck yourself.' At group she said that her goal was to get along better with people.

5/24 - She states she is not feeling well, so she did not attend groups. She cannot go on an outing because of last week's incident. She was congenial with staff and peers. She has not eaten and had Ensure for dinner. 'I don't want to eat. I just want a shake.' She is isolating.

5/25 - Mom brought lunch, cookies, soda, Ensure. Betsy is anxious about weight. She kept cigarettes in her room. She later was pleasant and agreeable to staff. She did chores, and she showered.

5/26 – She only had Ensure for breakfast and lunch, but she ate dinner. She read and wrote in her journal in her room.

5/27 – She was upset that she could not attend the NA meeting because of the "soda incident." She did not feel that was right and will bring it up at next ART meeting. She called the CM crying. She was not making progress, not participating, isolating. She was fine with staying on COT, as the team felt she was not ready.

5/28 – She had Ensure for the first 2 meals, watched comedy on TV, and phoned 4 times.

5/30 - Progress in attending groups. She felt sad and depressed, but likes living at TR. Therapy: she said she felt 'sad and angry because I am being grounded for being bad. Staff is abusive, brutal to me, and it's deteriorating my recovery. I think I may go back to Palo Verde or Sonora Hospital. I don't like rules.' She admitted to saying "fuck you" to staff and to calling police to tell them that she is being held at TR against her will. She also called her attorney to say she is being treated unfairly for rule violations. She also told her CM that she felt 'misused and abused' (one of Betsy's favorite phrases) due to staff conflicts. She requested a Judicial Review and was told that her behavior would impact her relationships in her life. She shared her journal and letters which admit to her having strong urges to drink. She journaled that she had learned distress tolerance skills which include using wise mind concepts of ACCEPTS: A. Activities; C. Contributing; C. Comparisons; E. Emotions; P. Pushing Away; T. Thoughts; S. Sensations; also self soothe with her 5 senses. She was sad and angry but was feeling better after this therapy session. She was reminded that she would need to follow rules to be regarded as trustworthy to go on outings.

At the ART meeting she was told that she would start her new medications soon. She would have blood work done and keep in touch with the doctor. She feels her mother controls her money. It was explained that her Social Security checks go to Project Home, her representative payee, who then distributes the money to her. It was explained that when she buys what she needs, she gives the receipts to her mother who then mails them to Project home. We discussed her goals: change way of thinking; maintain sobriety; stabilize on meds. She mentioned caffeine withdrawals and reducing her intake. She did a 'super awesome job cleaning the patio.' Pleasant behavior today.

5/31 - Sold cigarettes to peer. Staff talked about boundaries, rules, milieu, and putting an effort into things she struggles with. She thanked staff and agreed to share radio with peer.

June 2014, Betsy's Last Month

6/1 - Barn group cancelled because of heat advisory. She was told that drinking even non-caffeinated soda was not good for her. She did chores, ate meals, self-cued taking meds. She had no symptoms and attended community group. Her mother brought food for lunch and was medication compliant.

6/2 – She wants to go on Doxepin and Risperidal and go off Prolixin and Trazodone because they make her groggy when she awakes and cause disturbed sleep. She had few staff cues for medications, groups, and chores. She did not complete her chores, so staff had to complete them. She socialized with peers and listened to the radio. She had poor ADLs and was disheveled.

6/3 – She did not attend groups or do chores. She was lethargic and was isolated. She ate both meals. It was a very hot day. She did chores without cues and was thanked for her initiative. Her former poor behavior prohibited her from going to NA outside meeting. She self-administered medications and attended the community group. No ADLs, some anxiety, many questions.

6/4 – She attended all groups and ate her meals. She worked on this plan so she could attend outside meetings. She would lock up her purse. She thanked staff for helping her and kept asking, 'When are we going to Circle K?'

6/5 – She went to the library off site. She was compliant. The barn group was cancelled because of the heat.

6/6 – She redirected when she kept asking for coffee. She watched TV and read in her bedroom. She picked grapefruit or her mother.

6/7 – She had a good day. She went to Walmart and drank 2 milkshakes and did her chores. She swept the patio and picked up butts.

6/8 – She smoked during the night on the patio. She had 2 Aspirin for pain. She told her mother, 'Mom, I had a great visit with you.' She told her peers not to ask her for cigarettes. She stayed 1 whole hour at an AA meeting. She attended barn group.

6/9 – She did not complete her chores or follow her hygiene plan.

6/10 – She attended the Anger and Seeking Safety group. She did not complete ADLs even though cued by staff. She had body odor from not showering. She cleaned dishes without a prompt. She attended NA meeting.

6/11 – She went to barn group. She attended SMART recovery and Community meetings where she said she enjoyed NA meeting. She said that she needs re-evaluation for medications.

6/12 – She demonstrated positive energy. She attended all groups. She wanted to watch news on TV, and she was demonstrating progress toward her goals: to complete her chores such as cleaning the bathroom and her room; going on outings, such as going to the library, 'Of course, I want to go'; attending AA meetings. She really enjoyed hearing people speak and listening to the message 'One day at a time.'

6/13 – She had Ensure rather than breakfast. She was not terribly cooperative with staff. She was a bit defiant and did not want to engage or share what was bothering her. She had flat affect and was too late to attend barn group. The gate was closed.

6/14 – She could go on the bowling outing after her behavior the last time was discussed. She promised that there would not be a repeat of drinking or boundary issues and would follow staff's instructions. She was urged to take a shower and told staff she had, but she had not. She said, 'I really enjoyed going out. I just watched but I would like to play next time.' She had a poor conversation with her mother. 'I cannot deal with an 80 year old woman anymore.' She did chore and took her medications.

6/15 – She learned how to load the dishwasher, put in the soap, and handle food items with gloves. 'No one had ever showed me this.' She was low functioning, did not attend groups, and needed cues. She was upset about labeling personal food items. She agreed to be responsible for checking how much she had before accepting more snacks and drinks from her mother.

6/16 - Therapy session. Called her mother. Attended all groups. She was ADLs and was medication compliant. She was baseline functioning and had a good day.

6/17 – She shared with her CM, 'I am doing better than when I first came to The Ranch. I am less depressed.' She has not used alcohol since the 5/10 bowling incident. She has fair insight about MI and awareness as to when and why she is most triggered to drink or abuse medications. Her CM commended her about her areas of growth. She still complained about money and her mother, 'My payee is sending checks to my mother, and I don't have access to my own bank account. I want to be able to have my own money!' She disclosed that she believes she is ready to be discharged from The Ranch soon, and she contacted a friend with whom she might live. 'My Treatment is going well. I'm learning a lot. My favorite group is Equine therapy.' The CM said that we ended the session with ten deep, mindful breaths to achieve Mindfulness Based Stress Reduction. She thanked her CM. Betsy is attending groups, individual therapy and is superficially compliant. She was glad to see her mother at the doctor's appointment. She was cooperative when staff took her for lab work. She went to an NA meeting, and she said, 'It was really good.'

6/18 - Circle K outing, 'Why can't I buy beer. I am over 21 yrs old?'

6/19 - Barn group. She helped in washing and shampooing the horse. She combed and brushed the mane. 'I really like being around the horses.' She attended a 1 hour AA meeting, and it went well.

6/20 – She participated in all groups, functioning at baseline. 'It's gonna be a good day.' After listening to radio outside, she went on a library trip.

6/21 – She bought cookies during an outing to Walmart. She wants a soda every hour.

> ***6/21-*** *I can't write anymore. I want to end it; I can't go on. I wish it was over. This is* HELL!

6/22 – She watched soccer and then a movie on TV. She left the barn group early, and she tried to get points by saying it was cancelled. She brought trash to the disposal. Her mother brought items and lunch. She enjoyed the visit.

> ***6/22*** – *I weigh 137. I have low blood pressure from withdrawals from alcohol, medications, caffeine, soda. I have a change of diet with different food.*
> ***6/23*** *- I WANT TO DIE!*

6/23- She read a book and was polite to staff. She thanked them for dinner. 'It was delicious.'

6/24 – She likes to listen to music. She saw La Frontera 'tele-med.' At the NA meeting, 'I have been clean for 30 days now.' Staff praised her for this accomplishment and encouraged her to continue her efforts.

6/25 - ART meeting: Attending were Betsy, her mother, her therapist, the coordinator, and Genesis.

(NOTE: Genesis, her new case manager, was assigned to Betsy, and they met for the first time at this meeting. Betsy had really liked Jessica, her previous long term CM.)

Everyone agreed that she is doing very well at the moment. She has been engaging in groups and chores. They are continuing to work on unresolved grief, loss, SA, underlying issues, low self-esteem, shame and guilt. We discussed medications: possible decrease of Lithium and Hydroxyzine. We discussed the options of D/C or of staying longer which would require submitting another packet. She did not like hearing that, but she did not argue about it. She was unhappy at the thought of staying despite it being in her best interest. We discussed her behaviors and how she was engaging in treatment. She could be better with how she interacts with staff. She would like to live at Oasis, but due to an incident that occurred when she was last there, it is questionable.

She has been sober since May by attending NA and AA meetings. She is well groomed and dressed appropriately. Her mother is very involved in her treatment. She is experiencing stressors at The Ranch as she wants to D/C. She feels she is ready for D/C to a 2 bedroom house with a friend. She was informed that the longer she is in treatment the better chances for her being successful in recovery and that she was still early in recovery and had had a relapse while at

TR. By staying she would have more time to increase her coping skills to prevent relapse. Betsy did not respond well, hung her shoulders, and stopped smiling; 'Why? I am doing everything.' She was reminded of the drinking while on an outing. She hung her head and said 'OK.' CM suggested she find an AA sponsor, and she agreed.

She was not very happy with the outcome when asked how things were going. She questioned the 60 day extension to stay there. 'Fuck it; this is really fucked up.' She was very demanding and impatient when she came back from the ART meeting. She wanted to know exactly how many cigarettes she had left when she came. She could not get through on the phone, and could not leave the site. She expressed her feelings but understood the reasoning. She was anxious about staying longer but hopeful that she would remain clean and sober once she reached her goal of completing treatment.

6/26: THE FINAL DAY - Report from Behavioral Health Tech: Betsy was happy and singing along with the radio on the trip to the doctor's. Betsy went AWOL from her doctor's appointment that had been to check on lab results for her heart. (The results were not given then but were fine when her mother checked later.) After 45 minutes waiting, she was getting more and more impatient. Betsy said, 'I know they won't let me even go with you or for a walk. It's your fault that I got an extension. Don't do the same thing to my friend.' She was upset that her meds were decreased effective Saturday. I was sitting with Betsy and her mother. Betsy was getting so agitated with her mother that she told Betsy she was going to CVS for snacks. Betsy told me she was going outside to smoke. When her mother returned, Betsy was gone. She checked CVS, the gas station, and Tucson Medical Center. The Ranch called Rapid Reponse On-Call and Tucson Police Department. She had not been found. At 4:44pm TMC called to say she had been brought in to ER after 911 was called and 'was not well.' Her mother and sister arrived to find her dead.

In piecing together the facts, Betsy had gone to CVS and bought 2 boxes of Benadryl which she consumed behind the CVS in the wash. She was heard by a passer-by who called 911. The Hydroxyzine – Benadryl combination was lethal. She went into cardiac arrest and was DOA. Her mother went back to The Ranch for belongings later and thanked everyone. A HUGE SHOCK to everyone.

An Explanation

I supported the sixty day extension because I knew that as soon as Betsy went to a less structured living situation, she would go AWOL and succumb to her cravings for alcohol, Benadryl, etc. I couldn't condone that move knowing that she would be right back in the hospital again or else dead.

Betsy's final act explained in her own words

*Betsy wrote this on **2/17**, but it can be applied to the motivations underlying her final actions .*

For the relapse that brought me to Rosa Chante, I had gone to the Circle K and bought two cokes, two Reese's, one Pepsi, one Bacardi Gold Rum. Live and Let Live. Or should I say: Live and Let Die. The reasoning behind what I did – overdose – is simple: 'Keep It Simple.' I was reaching out my Spirit, crying out to God to make me as I am and release my Spirit from bondage of self – to let me rest in peace. NO MORE PAIN! That is basically the reasoning for what I did. Besides, I got feelings too. And I was sick of being used as the scapegoat who has to take the blame, even when it wasn't my fault, and I wasn't doing anything wrong just because things aren't quite righteously going their way, and I have to take the blame because I wasn't 'kissing their ass' and sucking up to them. That hurts. Then, being their doormat — something they can just walk over, literally. And then being their 'free-for-all,' being tossed around from here to there. Just pick me up and dump me off, so I am not in their way. FUCK YOU! All three of those things: Scapegoat; Doormat; and Free-For-All. All three led me into relapsing: taking too many medications, drinking, self-unworthiness, and no self-esteem. Baby Blue kitty cat and I have a lot in common: abuse, abandonment and neglect. You have come a long way, Baby Blue. Luv U! xxxOOO! I am very proud of Baby Blue. He is special.

House of Heart Assessment and Interviews

The following section includes interviews with the founders and the board members.

My Assessment

1. What is your connection? How did you come to HOH?

My daughter, Betsy, was diagnosed at the age of eighteen as Paranoid Schizophrenic, manic depressive and chronic substance abuser. Since she was thirteen, we knew something was very wrong. Subsequently, she was diagnosed as Dual Diagnosis: Schizoaffective and Chronic Substance Abuser. Beginning in 1980, she was hospitalized multiple times and treated inpatient and outpatient. By 2009, she had been placed in twenty-two group homes. The last one in 2009 was owned and rented to a church. Betsy was approached in a parking lot to come see the group home. The renter could not pay and was asked to leave. With her went all the clients but Betsy. The landlord agreed to rent us the home, after offering a young man the manager's position. That was how the House of Heart started.

The young man hired for the manager's position was bright and conscientious up to a point, and that point was reached when in afternoons we caught him 'doing meth.' He was fired, and we hired another friend of a friend, with a large heart. For almost a year, Betsy did reasonably well, with the pool, a garden, her cat and enough freedom to walk to the store. A member of our church invited two other women to live at the House of Heart as they were living hand-to-mouth with a bulldog and a cat. One of the women was exceptionally handy and helpful with maintenance, while the other had worked competently in a county group home for the elderly.

This arrangement worked for the House of Heart as the 'Sisterhood' of the Heart, based on 'The Four Agreements' by Don Luis Miguel. They are:
- *to speak impeccably*
- *always do your best*
- *do not make assumptions*
- *take nothing personally*

We held weekly meetings using a 'talking stick' which gave the residents a chance to share their wants and needs. They shared about what they could offer for the next week, what worked for them and what did not work. The meeting ended by saying the serenity prayer.

The CPSA (Community Partnership of Southern Arizona), the entity funded by the AZ Department of

Behavioral Health, oversaw agencies, such as: La Frontera (LFC), COPE and CODAC who checked us out, liking what they saw. They were impressed because the clients were involved in running the House. One client did the cooking. Two others were responsible for maintenance and the garden. Another client cleaned the bathrooms and they all cleaned their own rooms. The House did not have a car. Most transportation was dependent on my personal car. I drove frequently for shopping trips, picking up medications, trips to the doctors, or trips for fun.

Other residents came until we had a maximum of six clients at one time. Appropriate referrals kept being made until July 2013 when the agencies no longer referred high functioning SMI women. The only referrals from then on were the most complex clients who had failed to thrive in other settings. Our goal remained to be a Room and Board Home for women ages 45 to 65 with some form of mental illness. Presentations by mental health professionals were scheduled. Dinners were structured and family-style. Breakfast and lunch were not and clients were allowed access to food and to the refrigerator. Pets were encouraged, so that cats, dogs, and even a nomad parakeet who wandered into the pool area were welcomed and cherished.

2. What is your greatest joy? Disappointment?

My greatest joy was opening our hearts to those who had not received respect for many years and whose families had discarded them with little communication. To see the clients' enjoyment of gardening, caring for the pets, and sharing responsibilities in the home gave me a sense of making a difference in these women's lives. To see one 'sister' after another being chosen to be a 'Sister of the Heart,' having grown into that designation, was a reward in itself.

Another reward was seeing my friends from church engaged in becoming volunteers on our Advisory Board. Each one was involved with the residents, and they extended themselves repeatedly. Our friends attended House Meetings, functions, and holidays. They made their homes available to clients, and they took over the managerial duties when the HM and I were away. They donated not only time but money, goods, food, and LOVE.

My greatest disappointment was closing the house because during her stay at the HOH, Betsy had seven hospitalizations, multiple incidents with the law, several overdoses on her medications.

3. What worked for you or not?

The lack of finances worked against the HOH. We did not have sufficient income to hire a trained manager. The first manager left because of drugs. The next manager turned out to be an alcoholic and drug addict. The final manager had increasing problems of her own which impacted the house. We needed a trained professional to dispense medications which we could not afford. In addition, the amount of time that I spent transporting clients took a toll on me, my family, and the car.

I considered the strong personal and spiritual relationships that developed within the House (HOH) a success.

4. What would have helped to work better?

If I had not had my educational consulting practice which required quite a bit of travel, I would have had more time and energy to devote to the HOH. Not having a strong paid substitute when I was not available meant that the leadership was inconsistent.

5. Which of your expectations or needs were met or not?

I expected to see recovery, especially for Betsy, and that did not happen. Also it was difficult handling all of the requests for 'rides' to pick up food or medications. There were constant demands. I loved going to the House of Heart, and I enjoyed the residents, the laughter, and the 'collegiality.'

6. What was your overall experience? Would you do it again?

Under the system of complex referrals from agencies, I would not attempt to have six women who do not work outside the home cover the bills. The selection and screening process has to be much smoother. Because of my age, I would not try to run another B&C. The need is so great that I hope this book will propel others to go forward to do so.

7. What advice would you give someone wanting to start a group home?

1. Do all of the paperwork to become a 'nonprofit' ahead of time.
2. Check all licensing requirements carefully.
3. Look at the neighborhood and location so that public transportation and stores are easily available.
4. Have the Advisory Board set up ahead of time.

5. Identify and apply for possible grants ahead of time

8. What was the dream?

The dream was to create a high-quality home for women to relax and to realize they are accepted as they are and to help them find their potential and permanent joy in life.

9. Who are the people involved?

- Residents
- Landlord
- Advisory Board
- Managers
- Family

10. What are the categories to be evaluated ahead of time?

- Management: training, responsibility time, time off
- Location: pets, pool, garden
- Clients: diagnoses, range of severity, measurement of progress, family involvement
- Medication: how wide a range, how to dispense, how to pick up
- Chores: rotation, supervision: cleaning floors, bathrooms, own room, cooking, cleaning, substitutes if unable to do a chore

- Cooking: buying food, storing, preparation, serving, cleaning up
- Schedule: presentations, chores, fun, outings, meals, meds time, food bank
- Finances: good security, safe boxes, yard sales, donations
- Transportation: to the bank, cell phones, cigarettes, pets, outings, church, recreation.
- Guidelines: emergencies: steps to take
- Visitors: sign in and out
- Advisory Board: donations of time, clothing, furniture ,love
- Spiritual: Don Luis Miguel :*The Four Agreements*, develop community, sisterhood,
- Weekly house meetings: sharing with 'talking stick' the clients' wants, needs, and what one can offer.

Board Member Interviews

Board Member K

I came to assist friends Nancy and Rebecca as a volunteer in 2013 before the house closed in November 2013. I absolutely enjoyed my relationships with all the women residents and other volunteers, so much so that I am continuing to support one of them through housing and other needs. I called the HOH an Oasis which many troubled women could have used and could have had a fabulous experience. I appreciated that I was scheduled to work at regular times by helping in the garden or by bringing residents to the movies or to a Thanksgiving dinner. It would have helped if the residents were more prepared and on time for outings and appointments so we were not late. There should have been more follow-through, better communication and consistency, but I learned to roll with the punches.

I was disappointed in the slender stream of referrals which were insufficient to sustain the financial situation. There was never enough income to do what would have been best in all circumstances. What did not work for me was the turnover of residents, and some of the residents had to be asked to leave for unfortunate circumstances. If there had been a stronger river of applicants, there could have been a higher level of functioning and better consistency. The group could have been more compatible, and trust and respect more evident. The different levels of functioning meant real challenges.

All my needs and expectations were met. I wanted this service to be a regular part of my life, to stretch, and I found the house to be a quiet and orderly place for me and the women.

More houses like the HOH need to be started, with clear house rules and consequences, and with collaborative decision making. There is an enormous need for a calm, stable and safe place for troubled women. Location is important. In cases where clients suffer from alcoholism in addition to a CMI, the facility should not be close to a convenience store. Better transportation options would have been useful. Being informed of pitfalls for individual residents would have been helpful. For example, I was asked to stop at a fast food place on the way to a doctor's appointment, and the resident bought too much soda. If I had been informed that she had an issue of spending money on poor choices, I would have restricted her purchase. Guidelines would have helped. In one case, against house rules, a man was in a bedroom with a resident, and we had to work it out in the moment.

On the whole, I appreciated the support that Nancy and Rebecca gave me, and I know that the HOH helped many women.

Judy G

Other board members invited me. The founders provided a place for women with no other place to go. Everybody had 'skin' in the project and were treated equally. Each participant must be invested in their own and others' well-being if given responsibility to make something work. They volunteered for chores of their choosing and were active in their own treatment. I helped with transportation but it was difficult for me to get there. There were conflicts. Clients with extremely severe diagnosis were too disruptive at the HOH. The participants did not appear to understand 'The Four Agreements.' I liked the speakers and workshops. The garden was excellent. Everyone valued and learned from it, but the residents needed to do their assigned chores. I felt everyone should have been involved in making the rules, not just Rebecca and Nancy.

Barb M

Nancy had a dream to provide shelter for mid-aged women with no place to live. I was glad to participate. It was a joy to see how Nancy and Rebecca put the HOH together. Once a week, somebody came to teach the clients how to manage their lives more effectively, discussing feelings, alcoholism, addictions, and healing. I was pleased to be part of HOH. It was difficult with all of the clients' needs and the moving in and out of the HOH. The community was not developed, and there were too many dysfunctional clients who needed more support than we could give. There was chaos and always one or two who took up a lot of time and did not help each other. I got to know some of the clients quite well. I enjoyed their company. Assisting them gave me a sense of fulfillment. I knew when to say no and how to set boundaries. It was sometimes overwhelming for volunteers when we were called on to do more than possible. The HOH needed professional staff. Nancy and Rebecca were involved at the HOH day and night, and it was too much for them. They became exhausted. The HOH might have succeeded under more supervised circumstances. I believe in the concept behind the HOH. Betsy was the most dysfunctional. She took up a lot of Nancy's time and caused disruption in the group.

1. Advice: Start with endowments. Money was too tight. Rely on certain donations so no financial fallout when people move out.

2. Screening process needs to be tighter, not just who could afford, what kind of roles, expectation for them on how to participate, wonderful idea, some dreams are more fulfilling than others

Barb N

Nancy and Rebecca believed the HOH could be a safe, fun place for Betsy. I was asked to be a board member from the inception. I attended House meetings at least once a month. During the 'Circle meeting' we shared our concerns, and it was a safe place to share feelings. I took over house manager duties to allow the current HM to take a much needed vacation. She was the 24-7, chief cook and bottle washer, and she distributed medications. I took them to LFC and doctor appointments. I took them shopping or to pick up medications at CVS. I was the person to be called to help out when a need arose. I enjoyed keeping them all happy by cooking what they liked to eat, sitting and watching TV, talking, sharing, enjoying the garden. I did not swim. As a reformed smoker, being around so many smokers was difficult. The situation was difficult when clients had to leave or problems came up we could not handle. At the HOH the clients felt safe. It was a comfortable place to live. Rebecca and Nannie covered everything so well. There were good rules. The house was clean, floors, patio, and bathrooms. Some used their skills, cook, gardener, cleaning. Each had chores. My needs were met, but that was not the focus. Mine was to keep the clients safe and fed, to take them to appointments on time; and to keep them from not overdosing or getting too upset. I am happy and blessed that I do not have a chronic disability or an addictive personality. I have love and understanding for those who do suffer. I was fortunate enough to find a house as nice as the HOH. Financially, it was risky. I feel nothing but compassion for the clients at the HOH.

Interviews

Compilation of four volunteers' responses to the survey questions

Most of the volunteers were members of Sophia Circle at St. Francis in the Foothills who knew the struggles I had with my daughter for thirty years. They were aware I had a dream of establishing a house for middle-aged women, ages 45 to 65, who struggled with serious mental illness and life. They were drawn to the dream and wanted to participate. The greatest joy was seeing the house come together and how outside speakers came to discuss healing from alcoholism and addiction, as well as provide helpful techniques to the women to handle their lives more effectively. It was a great reward to see relationships built with all the residents and the enjoyment of serving them. House meetings were held at least twice a month. They used a talking stick, and the meetings were based on the principles of 'The Four Agreements' by Don Luis Miguel. In the meetings we shared where we were and our feelings. It was a safe time to share. One volunteer believed in the concept and took over for the manager who needed a vacation and or days off. She enjoyed the opportunity to relieve her for a much-earned vacation from being chief cook and bottle washer, distributor of medications and supervisor of cleaning. She loved keeping everybody happy, cooking what they liked to eat, sitting and watching TV with them, enjoying the garden, talking, and sharing.

One disappointment was the slender stream of referrals resulting in a shortage of money. In the last few months, July to November 2013, we took many inappropriate referrals. Serious problems came up that we were not equipped to handle so we asked some women to leave. They felt the house was safe and a comfortable place to live: an OASIS. The residents moving in and out disrupted the community and made it cumbersome and chaotic. Not everyone was supportive and helpful to each other. A few residents took up all of the time. We needed to be more realistic about whom we accepted, and we needed more appropriate referrals from the agencies, La Frontera, CODAC, and COPE. Another disappointment was some residents did not follow through with their commitment to meet and be ready to go to the movies or shopping. It was frustrating for the volunteers, who learned to 'roll with the punches.' A volunteer who was a reformed smoker believed the smoking was a 'waste of time ,money, and lungs.'

The volunteers who felt fulfilled learned to say ' no' to requests that could be overwhelming. The HOH needed a stronger stream of applicants so that we could afford a professional manager. We were called on "day and night" and it was too much. Nancy and Rebecca were weary. All liked the rules helping residents to do their chores, the housecleaning, sweeping floors and patio, cleaning bathrooms. Some of the residents enjoyed using their skills for cooking and gardening. Each of the clients was invested. Some of the volunteers offered Thanksgiving dinner and stretched themselves to assist the residents, using their experience. The volunteers believed the House worked well and were available when needed.

The decision-making team was strong. One volunteer suggested more investments from the residents. Everybody had 'skin' in the project. They felt empowered to do their very best. They were guided rather than treated, and the Budget should be prepared by the members which lends itself to a purposeful life with good support. Everyone was aware that the severity of the mental illness of some members caused repetitive acting out behavior which was a hindrance to the total cohesiveness of the house. All liked the house location but thought it could have been closer to a bus line and stores. Our advice is to start with an endowment and enough money so the screening process could be tighter. On the whole, the dream was only partially fulfilled and the house had to close. Having a place for women struggling to find themselves is a concept to be pursued.

Client Interview

Client M

The House of Heart was a great fit. There was joy, friends and fun. I had forgotten how to have fun. Negative things happened because there were unhealthy women. I suggested ways things could change. I felt frustration with the situation. On the positive side, I loved the house meetings which gave everyone the opportunity to express their feelings and their thoughts in a safe way. The food was not healthy, and I was hoping to stay healthy. Rebecca, Nancy, and the HM talked about issues. There were problems because new women kept coming in and sometimes the problems were unmanageable. More open discussion about options to solve problems would have been good. My expectations were not met. I needed a house without addicts or alcoholics. I needed a safer, less stressful environment. Rebecca and Nancy were always available 'beyond measure for anything.' I thank them for that. There were outlets for creativity like the garden which awakened something I had forgotten I had. If I were to do it again, I would know what questions to ask. Are there any active alcoholics, addicts, or uncontrolled SMI? There was one who was not stable. It is devastating if uncontrolled. I would ask about food and diet. I would also ask about the home and about rent, food, and budget. How does it work? I would need to know what was going on with my money. I would ask to be introduced to all the participants before I moved in to get a sense of safety and to see how I feel. I would do a background check on each resident to see if there are any legal issues, even though background checks costs money, to avoid serious conflict down the line. I felt frustrated with those who did not take their medication. Clients should not be allowed to isolate themselves in their rooms to watch TV. There needs to be more outings and community service as a community. The 'Four Agreements' are a 'fabulous way to run a home.' I still have mine posted. The medication box should be in a safe place. We did major shopping at Costco and the grocery store for fresh food. It is important to use the food it and not let it 'go bad.' There are opportunities at the Food Bank and the Market on the Move for great food. Deliveries of weekly sweets were 'overkill' and too tempting. They were distracting on the counter. Having pets was a wonderful idea, making the house homey and loving. They were well taken care of with responsible owners. Transportation was available, and Nancy and Rebecca were there when needed. The house needed to be close to stores.

Fate of House of Heart

In July 2013 the State shut down most of the B&C facilities in Tucson except for House of Heart because La Frontera, COPE, CODAC set up their own B&C facilities for less complex cases. As a result, the former B&C facilities closed, and the number of B&C facilities, now administered by La Frontera, COPE and CODAC was drastically reduced. The House of Heart remained open, but the only cases referred were the most difficult and complex. Without the funding or staffing to handle such difficult cases, the House of Heart closed in November 2013.

A Sister's Experience

The monologue by George Clooney's character at the beginning of "Descendants" explains that everyone assumes life must be easier because of Hawaii's blue skies and beautiful beaches, but in fact life can be as hard or harder. I think of that misunderstanding when considering my family's move from Philadelphia, PA to Tucson, AZ in the summer of 1971. Our family's unresolved pain, grief and anger burrowed deeper in the warmth and sunlight. Those emotions became more insistent and could not be ignored until eventually they evolved into the poison of addiction and illness and had to be brought into the open.

My parents drove the family station wagon across the country from Philadelphia to Tucson filled with the remnants of an entire life lived in the Philadelphia area, along with our black Labrador, Samantha. My father started a private practice as a Neurologist. My mother eventually became the headmaster of a small country day school.

The miles slipped by during their trip because Betsy, age 9, and I, age 10, weren't with them. In the evenings, after a long hot day of driving without air conditioning, they would smuggle Samantha into their motel room, ignoring the "No Dogs" sign. My father, mother and Samantha arrived at 9020 E. Eagle Feather before the moving van and before the plane carrying Betsy and me. Betsy and I arrived before the moving van which carried all of the furniture. The pool, nestled between the "L" shape of our thick-walled house, was home to long strings of Colorado River Toad eggs extending downwards like miniature kelp threads. The summer monsoon season saw the Colorado River Toads laying their eggs in any source of water they could find, and they considered our pool an excellent place for reproduction. As Tucson developed and pushed the desert farther from our house, the toads disappeared. Inside the empty house we easily identified and avoided the scorpions hiding in the corners of the bedrooms. Betsy and I wondered at this new country that was our new home. But we had each other and would face the adventure together.

Betsy and I, close in age, were inseparable, and we had honed each other's skills at Jacks, Chinese Jump Rope, Crazy Eights, and every other activity that two siblings close in age participated in during the late 1960's in the greater Philadelphia region. I tried to keep one step ahead of Betsy and succeeded academically but not socially, athletically, or musically. Betsy stood taller than I by four or five inches, with much of that height in her long straight legs, and unlike me she was never overweight as a child. Her large, luminous hazel eyes were full of humor, fun and mischief, matched only by her wide and ready smile. Some said she looked like Caroline Kennedy.

During the first few years in Tucson, we continued as each other's closest companion. We spent long afternoons swimming in the pool that had been home to the Colorado River Toad eggs, playing Marco Polo and other fun pool games wiling away hours in the Arizona sun, emerging from the water toasted as browned nuts. Surrounded by cousins, we continued tanning and developing our swimming, tennis, bicycling, sailing, and card skills during our summer visits to Martha's Vineyard and other places on the East Coast. Betsy and I, with help from our mother, made candles from the "boots" of downed Saguaro cacti. We would scour the desert for the dried Saguaro ribs and then look closer for the rounded out scars where animals and birds had burrowed into the cactus for shelter while it was alive. The rounded shape of the dried scarred "boot" made excellent shapes for candles. Our mother made sure we were confirmed in the Episcopal Church, which we did together. Betsy and I hiked and played tennis, but horseback riding took up most of our afternoons. During the summer, we would ride in the morning to escape the relentless heat of the southern Arizona summer. Betsy excelled in ways I could only hope for, and she and her horse, Patches, had fun and competed successfully.

We lived a life full of privilege, but threads of darkness had woven into the fabric of our lives by the time we moved to Tucson; alcoholism, mental illness, suicide, and painful memories. My father disliked the public face of Christianity and did not practice any faith or spirituality. My mother, Betsy and I attended church until Betsy and I reached junior high school. After that, neither Betsy nor I attended church. An older cousin, who embraced all of the rebellion of the 1960's influenced Betsy and me, making the drug culture appear glamorous. She exposed Betsy and me to readings about witchcraft and black magic which affected Betsy, especially, and terrified her as a young child. By the time we moved to Tucson, Betsy and I viewed alcohol, drugs, and rebellion as both acceptable and desirable if we wanted to be "cool." In Tucson, with the prevailing permissive culture of the 1960's and 1970's, everyone we knew had easy access to cigarettes, alcohol, drugs, sex, and rebellion. Betsy and I were no exception. Maybe Betsy became trapped in addiction to self-medicate a latent mental illness or maybe she just liked alcohol, cigarettes, and drugs. Whatever the initial reason, she remained addicted for the rest of her life, and by sixteen she experienced her first psychotic break. Unlike Betsy, I disliked drinking alcohol or taking drugs, but I did like food and rebellion. I have struggled with eating all my life, but my rebellion was limited to not respecting my parents, to piercing one ear, and to reading books like "A Diet for A Small Planet" and the "The Autobiography of Malcolm X."

My life and Betsy's life diverged considerably from that point. Losing Betsy to mental illness and chemical dependency was a loss so painful that I am still processing it. As the mental illness and chemical dependency took further hold of Betsy, the sister I had known disappeared, replaced by someone overwhelmed by the severity of her condition. It took many years for me to accept and love my sister as an

ill and addicted person and to stop grieving for the
sister I hoped to grow up with.

My life progressed. I went on to college, taught
English in China, and then went to graduate school.
I met my husband in graduate school, married,
moved away from Tucson, and had three daughters.
Despite this seemingly "normal" progression, I have
had struggles. I struggled in college (1978-1983) and
have experienced depression and anxiety on and off
over the years. Maintaining a consistent and healthy
weight is difficult. During this time period, life for
Betsy was nightmarish. She had multiple
hospitalizations, attempted many treatment
programs, changed residences often, attempted
suicide, was homeless, suffered and inflicted
physical abuse, was hit by a car, went to prison. Her
addiction and mental illness became progressively
worse as she grew older. Over the years I visited and
communicated with Betsy as much as I could, and I
tried to help my mother with Betsy's treatment and
care, as my father became less and less involved with
Betsy as the years progressed.

There was two other times when our adult lives
overlapped significantly. Betsy was the maid of
honor at my wedding, and I was so proud of her and
happy that she wanted to be my maid of honor,
knowing how difficult it was for her. Then, when
my oldest child was seven months old, Betsy gave

birth to a wonderful and healthy boy. Because of Betsy's mental illness and addiction, her son was taken from her immediately. My husband and I raised him along with our seven month old daughter for the first fourteen months of his life at which time my father's first cousin adopted him. My sister never saw him again, but she never forgot him. Whenever she and I talked or visited, she would ask if I had news about her son. Betsy experienced terrible events in her life that caused her pain, loss and anger, but nothing was as bad as losing her son. She never recovered from the pain, loss, and anger.

The HOH was one of the many places Betsy lived over the years, but it was one of the most home-like. She enjoyed the pool, the garden, and the back porch where she and the other clients could smoke. She liked having her cat, Baby Blue, with her, and she had easy access to a local park for her daily walks. There were always regular meals, and the house was clean. She enjoyed seeing my mother and the co-founder, Rebecca, on a regular basis. When I visited Tucson, I visited Betsy and became familiar with how the house was run, and got to know the other clients. My mother and Rebecca kept me informed of the struggles and victories at the HOH, which clearly occupied most of their time and money. Despite how much Betsy liked the HOH, her addictions drove her to take advantage of the more relaxed and home-like atmosphere of the HOH by panhandling at the shopping center, buying beer, and getting drunk. She used the money to buy stronger liquor and Benadryl to get high. Once she started drinking or taking drugs, she became rude, abusive, paranoid and angry because the alcohol and/or drugs interfered with her prescription medications. Betsy was not alone among the clients to abuse substances or be unmanageable. Some of the clients, including Betsy, had to leave either temporarily or permanently as a result of untenable behavior. The HOH housed women who struggled most of their lives with mental illness and addictions – a very difficult population. I am not sure what would have helped the HOH stay in operation, but a regular funding source and well-trained staff would have been a good start. I am glad the HOH was available to Betsy for the years 2009 to 2013.

After the relative stability of the HOH, Betsy began a downward spiral of overdoses and hospitalizations, culminating in her death on June 26, 2014. The years of addiction and illness took a terrible toll on her. It was not clear either to Betsy, my mother or to me if the overdosing was due to the brutal and unforgiving cravings of Betsy's addictions or to a desire to end her life. By the end of 2013 Betsy was living in yet another halfway house. When I went to visit her, she wore an over-sized blue t-shirt that hung low over her pants. The University of Arizona and Wisconsin game was playing in the background. Her hair was down, and silver strands sprinkled the deep brunette hair. The ends were uneven and untrimmed. Hers was the face of the nameless homeless women I have seen anywhere and everywhere and who seem less than human, but in this case I knew her and could name her, "**Elizabeth Barnes Masland**," my sister, whom I have loved and cherished. Occasionally, in her agitated state, she pushed her sleeves up to her shoulders revealing a deep scar running the length of her bicep, the result of being hit by a car several years back. She talked about heaven and hell, and while she talked I saw how yellowed and stained her teeth had become. Two of her bottom teeth were missing. She talked about our childhood home, sometimes apologizing for her behavior, crying and then not crying, angry and yet contrite. Her deeply lined tanned face reflected the hours in the sun panhandling for change to feed her addictions or from walking around the local park or from spending days homeless. Betsy's eyes, still deep and luminous, looked at me, pleading for me to take her home, away from the halfway house where she had been sent after her latest overdose. Betsy is fourteen months younger than I am, but she looked twenty years older. If Betsy only had to deal with an addiction or only with a mental illness and if our home life had been different, she might have had a chance to lead a "normal" life filled with joy, love, and light. As it was, Betsy died alone on a bright sunny day in Tucson in a small wash next to a drug store, having consumed two boxes of Benadryl, causing a deadly interaction with her prescribed medication. My sister, my sister, my sister, I am so sorry, and I miss you.

Conclusion

So be it: The tale of my daughter's struggles through the threshold of life with SMI and Chronic Substance abuse. I trust that by sharing the details of her joys and anguish, from the many viewpoints - her biographical and family history, her journal, her medical, psychological, and residential records, the interviews of Board Members and residents of the last House she lived in - that some of the pitfalls and obstacles she and the family experienced with the Mental Health System, as well as with her brain disease and addiction are highlighted. As a result, the journey may be easier for both the family and the one suffering. We hope so. Our daughter was my greatest trial, but she was the greatest contributor to my personal growth, forcing me to reach my best self, and to serve others. As a Co-founder of PLAN, NAMISA, NAMI of AZ, as well as a Support Group at my church, I am now sought after as a Consultant to help other families cope with a family member, a founder of the House of Heart and Heartbreak. Betsy forged my path. My gratitude to her, even though I could not ease her journey, she has given me the tools to be of service to others. The heartbreak is not over, it may never be. With the diligence, competency and compassion of her older sister, and Rebecca, this book has been birthed. Thresholds of your life will be transported to much higher levels than you could have imagined.

Glossary

- 1:1 therapy – One on one therapy
- AA – Alcoholics Anonymous
- ACCM – Agency of Case Managers in the 1980s
- ADAPT – Former regional behavioral entity which became CPSA and then became CENPATICO in 10/1/2016. This is the agency that the AZ State chooses to dispense monies to agencies, such as the following: La Frontera Center, CODAC, COPE, HOPE, Inter-Mountain
- ADL – Activities of Daily Living
- AHCCS – Arizona State Health Insurance
- Akathesia – Dry mouth from medications
- ART – All Residential Treatment Staffing
- ASH – AZ State Psychiatric Hospital in Phoenix
- AWOL – Away without leave
- B&C – Board and Care. In July, 2014 the state shut most down except for House of Heart because La Frontera, COPE, CODAC set up their own board and care facilities. Only the most difficult cases were referred to House of Heart.
- Bridge, Medication – Order prescription medications until due date for next pickup

- Cenpatico – New name for the Regional Behavioral Health Agency RBHA
- CDV – Casa de Vida, a sober living center owned by La Frontera
- CM - Case Manager
- CODAC – Tucson Mental Health Agency
- COMPASS – Substance abuse crisis center
- Co-Dependent – See the definition for Enable
- COT – Court Ordered Treatment
- CPES – Mental health agency in the 1980s
- CPS – Child Protective Services
- CPSA - Community Partnership of Southern Arizona
- CR – Crisis Respite
- CRC - Crisis Response Center
- D/C – Discharge
- DD – Developmentally Delayed
- DIP – Drinking in Public
- DP – Depression
- DTS – Danger to Self
- DTO – Danger to Others
- Dual Diagnosis – Mental Illness and Substance Abuse
- DUI – Driving Under the Influence
- DV – Domestic Violence
- Enable – to give into others' addictive wants, not their healthy needs
- ER – Emergency Room

- ETOH – Alcohol
- EW – Empowering Women
- GD – Gravely Disabled
- Group C – A LFC group that focused on Compassion, Conflict Resolution, Control and other positive behaviors
- GSA – Guardianships of Southern Arizona
- HI – Harmful ediation
- HM – House Manager
- HOH – House of Heart, the group home administered by Betsy's mother and by her mother's friend, Rebecca Redelsheimer.
- HOPE – Tucson Mental Health Agency
- HUD – Department of Housing and Urban Development
- ICE – alcoholic beverage
- IL – Independent Living
- Intermountain – Tucson Mental Health Agency
- IP - Involuntary Petition, Title 6 – a person has to be placed in a restrictive environment for their sake and the sake of others.
- LFC - La Frontera Center, an agency that dispenses mental health treatment in Pima County.
- LARC – Was a drug and alcohol treatment center for women. LARC became New Directions

- MAC team – Mobile Acute Care that comes to assess violence, crisis, and to transport to the hospital if needed
- Meds - Medications
- Medical Bridge – fill in prescription medications until date for next medication pick up
- MHC – Mental Health Center
- MH Diversion – Mental Health diversion plan that would take the place of serving jail time
- MR – Mt Rose – one of the houses at Thornydale Ranch
- NA – Narcotics Anonymous
- NAMI – National Alliance for the Mentally Ill
- NAMISA – National Alliance for the Mentally Ill of Southern Arizona
- ND – New Directions
- Nueva Luz – Group Home
- NW Hospital – Northwest Hospital
- OP – Outpatient
- PAD - Persistently Acutely Disabled
- Pasadera – On October 16, 2016 Pasadera took over for SAMHC
- PCP – Primary Care Physician
- Peer – Person with SMI/Chronic substance abuse

- PHF – Psychiatric Health Facility - a Level I lock down facility, a step down from the hospital
- PLAN - Planned Lifetime Assistance Network
- PRN – Patient Request Now
- Protect – to rescue from consequences of their actions
- RBHA – Regional Behavioral Health Agency – Chosen by AZ Dept. of Behavioral Health as the entity to distribute funds to agencies.
- Revoked/Revocation – privileges are taken way. COT would be implemented to take Betsy to a more restricted placement.
- Rosa Chante's – a locked down assisted living home targeting dementia or Alzheimer patients. Recommended by the law firm, Bogutz and Gordon.
- RF – Recovery Facility
- RP – Relapse Prevention
- ROI – Request for Information
- RC or Rosa's – Rosa Chante House – a house dedicated to Alzheimer and Dementia patients. It is a lock down facility.
- RP – Relapse Prevention
- SA – Substance Abuse
- SA – Suicide Attempt
- SA Ed – Substance Abuse Education

- Safety Plan – A plan that is cooperatively designed by therapist and client
- SAMHC – Southern Arizona Mental Health Center which became Pasadera, the crisis clearing center for the involuntary petitions for hospitalization
- SAMHSA – Substance Abuse and Mental Health Services Administration
- Serenity Prayer – AA prayer "God grant me the Serenity..."
- SI – Suicidal Ideation
- SLS – Sober Living Setting
- SMART- Safety Management of Alcohol Recovery Treatment – alternative program for substance abusers
- SMI – Severe Mental Illness, formerly CMI or Chronic Mental Illness
- SO – Significant Other
- SSA – Social Security Administration
- SSI – Social Security Insurance
- Tardive Dyskinesia – tremors from medications
- The Institute for Living – A renowned psychiatric hospital in Hartford, CT
- TR – Thornydale Ranch – a Level II facility owned by La Frontera
- TMC (Tucson Medical Center)
- Twelve Step Program – AA program for Alcoholics

- UMC – University Medical Center
- Chart of History of Tucson Service Providers (see Glossary)

1980 - ACCM →ADAPT →CPES

1990-2016 - CPSA→La Frontera→ Cope→ Codac→ Intermountain

2016 - Cenpatico→HOPE→ CPI

2016 - Department of Behavioral Health Services→AHCCCS

APPENDIX I – Betsy's Timeline
Chronology of Events in Betsy's life

1973 - Puberty, behavior problems, mood swings, cognitive processing difficulties, lack of impulse control, alcohol abuse begins. Suspended from Green Fields Country Day School where her mother was Principal.

1976 - Expelled from school. DUI – Her license was taken away.

1977 - Attended Miss Porter's School (psychologist on board) and was expelled.

1978 - Maternal grandmother and maternal uncle both died this year. The funeral for Betsy's maternal grandmother was on Betsy's 16th birthday.

5/8/1978 –
- Graduated from Special Projects, Tucson High School. Worked during the summer for the Youth Conservation Corps.
- Diagnosed with Bi-Polar and Paranoid Schizophrenia
- Hospitalized at Palo Verde Hospital for six weeks. Dr. Schorsh was the physician. Her medications included: Stellazine and Lithium

- First psychotic break while vacationing on Martha's Vineyard Island, MA. She had auditory hallucinations and her behavior was erratic.
- She was hospitalized involuntarily in Tucson, AZ at Daybreak and Palo Verde Hospital until the insurance ran out.
- Betsy started taking illicit street drugs.

1979-
- Finished 1st semester at Pima Community College
- LFC- Vocational Rehab six months
- Drunk in Public
- Her medications included Elavil with some improvement, and then it stopped working.
- Betsy ran away by bus to Tucumcari, NM

1980 - 1981 –
- Entered the Institute for Living, a psychiatric hospital in Hartford , CT
- Medications included: Stellazine, Haldol, Prolixin: Imipramine, Fluphenazine

1980 - 1983 - Mom left Tucson and worked in the East.

7/82 - Betsy stepped down to an AA program, but her behavior was not normal.

1 - 4/1982 - Yale-New Haven Clinical Research

4/82-2/83 - Gould Farm, MA

7-8/82 – Falmouth and Martha's Vineyard, MA

1/83 - 11/83 –Tucson, AZ - Kiva House(Intermountain) She was evicted because of alcohol abuse and a co-dependent relationship with her SO. She was on ACCHS.

1/1983 - Both mother and Betsy flew home to Tucson. She cut her wrists and was hospitalized ten times at Kino Hospital in Tucson, AZ.

10/84-12/84 Omega House

12/84- 12/85 La Llave - (La Frontera)

1985 - Diagnosed Schizoaffective with Chronic Substance Abuse

1/25/88 - Judge Alice Truman explained Guardianship. Probate Court, Arizona Title 12-2451. Parents are not responsible for mentally disabled children after they turn eighteen. Public Fiduciary takes over conservatorship if there is no interested choice for a person in need of protection or is incapacitated. Title 14: Guardianship - letters are necessary for a temporary order. Cannot place mentally ill patient in psychiatric facility, so they must go to the County and file a legal petition. There is limited guardianship, a less restrictive possibility. The process to file petition, includes giving fourteen days' notice, making the correct allegations and developing annual reports. There is national interest in reforming Guardianship laws. In 1987 in AZ, there were 916 guardianships, 625 minors, 79 adults. Title 14 does not terminate unless a petition showing the client cannot make responsible decisions is filed, the ward dies or the court terminates. Title 36-provided limited time guardianship. COT could be invoked if DTS, DTO, PAD, or chronically disabled. The will is probated when client dies with Court and lawyer fees owed.

11/85-2/86 - Vocational Rehabilitation at the Sheltered Workshop

12/1988 – Was imprisoned for Domestic Violence. Hospitalized at Kino Hospital.

3/89 – 1990 – My husband created the Guardianships of Southern Arizona to assist with guardianship for the chronically mentally ill.

3/1993 – Entered Compass Mental Health LLC to detox from Crack. She became anorexic.

3/5/93 - James, Betsy's son, was born after a difficult delivery. CPS took him away from Betsy while still in the hospital. Betsy's sister and husband took care of him along with their own seven month old daughter for fourteen months, at which time James was adopted by relatives.

1996-2000 – Betsy lived in Tucson House, a HUD facility. She was evicted and ineligible for other conventional housing until 2005.

9-11/02 – CDV (went AWOL)

12/02 - COT- OP treatment and if failure go to hospital

12/02 – **Seven** days involuntary in Palo Verde Hospital because she was psychotic

3/03 – Betsy ran away from CDV. Involuntary COT implemented and went to Kino Hospital.

1/25/03 - In Kino discharged to Casa Alegre

7/04 - Domestic Violence citation –twice

1/05 – Admitted to Kino Hospital and then Casa Alegre.

1/05 –2/06 - Mental Health Diversion program – COT.

5/27/05 – Kino Hospital

6/07 - Involuntary = PAD Persistent / Acute Disability

8/07 - Drinking in Public, trespassing; failure to appear, COT, **LARK** (now New Directions) scared her because of heroin addicts screaming & demanding cigarettes.

10/2008 –Mammogram lump;

11/25 - Breast biopsy is negative

3/08 - CDV

2/27/09 - TMC ER

3/23/09 - AWOL –Crisis bed COMPASS

3/27/09 - TMC

4/09 - Picked up last night for DIP, littering, misdemeanor. Bond posted for $100 cash. Sixty-one police records on Betsy.

4/23-4 - UMC Hospital

5/26/09 – In Tucson City Court she was fined $162 for failure to yield to truck. Her left humerus bone was fractured when hit by the car.

6/29/09 - TMC ER Head Injury

7/2/09 - Refused diagnostic mammogram

8/11/09 - Refused GYN appointments. CPSA Complaint

9/09 - CPSA Video Court in Kino - COT dropped as per client.

10/16/09 - TPD took Betsy to St. Josephs.

1/14/10 - Reasons for COT: inability to self-regulate, prescription meds, OTC meds (eg. Ibuprofen), caffeine intake excessive –hypernatremia, alcohol abuse, finances, inappropriate use of alcohol, sells cigarettes, temper/abusive language, sleep patterns, personal safety, eating disorder, fills up with soda & refuses to eat

7/10- Criminal trespassing: if charges are dropped she goes to Kino and cannot be released. CPSA has a jail liaison

9/10 - City Court- Bond $100 for littering/polluting, DIP –Drunk in Public and twice failure to appear

7/21/13 - Involuntary application for Title 36 petition while at HOH because of DTS and DTO.

1982 - 2014
35 Residence Changes / Hospitalizations:

- Yale New Haven Clinic, CT
- Falmouth, MA
- UPH Kino
- CRC-
- Palo Verde
- Sonora
- Institute for Living
- UMC - University Medical Center
- TMC - Tucson Medical Center
- St. Joseph's Hospital
- Gould Farm, MA
- Kiva House
- Omega House
- La LLave
- LARC
- Agape
- La Fiesta McDaniel's House
- 3351 N. Overton Heights
- Adobe Manor Mobile Home
- Ana's Home
- Tucson House
- Eagle Crest
- Safe Haven
- Casa Alegre
- Mountain Rose
- New Directions

- Casa de Vida
- Mountain Rose
- Oasis
- PHF
- Rosa's Chante
- Thornydale Ranch
- Mt. View
- House of Heart
- Rosa's Chante
- Thornydale Ranch
- House of Heart

APPENDIX II – HOH Sample Calendar

2011-

7/10   Resident A. goes to work and then to a CODAC appointment

8/26   Board Member I. in charge at HOH

9/6   Resident B. goes to court (Rebecca takes)

10/7   Resident C. goes to doctor's appointment

10/15   Found rats in kitchen closet

11/8   Resident C has a doctor's appointment

2012-

2/7   Resident D. appointment at LFC

2/8   Inspection by LFC. Safety and cleanliness-passed

2/23   Resident D. goes to LFC

3/7   Passed LFC Inspection

3/19   Resident D. appointment at LFC

4/2   Resident D. appointment at LFC

4/16   Resident D. appointment at LFC

5/1   Resident D. appointment at LFC

5/14   Resident D. appointment at LFC

6/12   Resident D. appointment at LFC

7/11   Resident B., D. and E. appointments at LFC

8/9   Resident B. and dog - appointment

8/17   Resident B. appointment

9/19   Resident D. appointment at LFC

9/20	New Resident for HOH. Resident F.
10/3	Resident D. appointment at LFC
11/1	Resident D. appointment at LFC
11/3	LFC Mental Health Support group
11/29	New Resident G. arrives at HOH

12/20 Attend Church Christmas for Homeless-Operation Deep Freeze

2013-

1/3	Residents B., G., H., I. appointments
1/13	Resident B. Birthday
1/15	Resident D. Birthday
2/22	New Resident J. appointment
3/1	New Resident J. appointment
4/23	Resident F. Birthday
5/26	Resident K. Birthday
6/1	New House Manager, $50 an hour.

7/1-10 HM away; Carpet cleaning

8/16	Movie outing
8/18	Resident L. appointment at TROT -

Nancy drive

8/30	Board Member B. drove to movies
9/5	House Meeting at owner's home
9/14	Yard Sale

10/26 Resident L.'s birthday-Pinnacle Peak

10/29 Resident J. moves out

11/12	Res D. LFC

APPENDIX III – Index for HOH notebook (locked in safe)

- List of places of residences and medical records
- MH Articles, AA
- AHCCS Insurance forms
- CPSA (Community Partnerships Of S AZ-former funding entity until 10/15)
- Creative Responses for Conflict Resolution-Grace Rich
- Brain Tissue Donation form
- Dental- El Rio, St. Elizabeth's Clinic
- DES (Dept. of Economic Security- Food stamps)-Family Assistance
- Eating resources- pizza, etc.
- EFT- (Emotional Feeling Touch- Mary Stafford)
- Hospitals- TMC , UPH Kino
- Hyperkalemia
- Housing
- Medical Issues
- NAMI (National Alliance of Mental Illness, NAMISA of S AZ)
- La Frontera Center (LFC)
- PLAN-(Planned Lifetime Assistance Network- care during /after parent life)
- SAMHC (S AZ Mental Health Coordinator) Crisis line 622-6000
- Schizophrenia
- Social Security Association- SSA- SSI (Income)

APPENDIX IV – Betsy's files which she kept in a suitcase

- Address changes
- APIPA- AZ Physicians Insurance Patient Assistance
- DES- Dept. of Economic Security
- Family Correspondence
- La Frontera (LFC) classes- Self-Esteem, Anger, Women's Issues, Relapse Prevention
- Legal - Court, petitions, arrests
- Medications,
- Pets: Casper, Baby Blue
- Project H.O.M.E.
- SMART Recovery
- TMC Healthcare
- UPH (United Health care) Kino
- PHF -Level 2- the 'Puff'

~~~~~~~~~~~~~~~~~~~~~~~~~~~~~~~~

APPENDIX V - Games

- Twelve C's: Confidence, confession, conviction, conversion, continuance
- All is well: Acceptance, Self-Awareness, Practice Principles, Primary Purpose
- Take yourself lightly
- GET TO KNOW YOU GAMES:
  - Names
  - Alligator- trust, respect, love, faith
  - How important are the following in your life: 1-10
    - Personal happiness
    - Happy family life
    - Live life my own way
    - Change world for the better
    - Live and work in the world of ideas
    - Make life-long friendships
    - Understand others
    - Stand up for my own rights
    - Perform/Create works of art
    - $
    - Service to others
    - Active in politics
    - BE important and successful
    - Religion
    - Tell truth even if it hurts others
    - Be married
    - Be conformist

- Pair off:
  - How can your respect for society's rules, as a citizen, cope effectively with the outside world?
  - The way I make contact with someone new is to...
  - The way I feel about what we are doing now is...
  - The way I feel now is...
  - When I am anxious I...
  - The most threatening thing for me to do with others is...
  - The nicest thing about me is...
  - It is hard for me to talk about...
  - Donut
  - Sat Nam

ABOUT THE AUTHOR

Nancy Potts Masland, MS ED. and Ed.S (Special Education: Emotional Development, Learning disabilities, and Gifted.)

For thirty years, Nancy was considered ' a giant' in the field of independent Educational Consulting, counseling children, youth and adults. She taught, counseled and administered both day and boarding schools in the East and West. In 1983, she founded Nancy P. Masland and Associates to offer a personalized educational consulting service and mentor new consultants. In 2012, she won the nationally prestigious Katz Award for Community Service at the Independent Educational Consultants Association, and in 2015, the first Calo award in recognition of her unparalleled compassion, thoughtful guidance and vigorous community support. CALO is a member of the National Association of Therapeutic Schools and Programs. Nancy is on the Advisory Boards of the Abbie School (for autistic children), NAMISA and PLAN, of which she was a founding member, and the Green Fields Country Day School. She was the first President of

NAMI of AZ. She is currently on the Mental Health Ministry of St. Francis in the Foothills Church, and the Community Advisory Committee for Cenpatico. As Co-President of her Bryn Mawr College Class, and a founding member of an elders group, Nancy brings her experience as an Interfaith Spiritual Director to lead Memorial Services.

As founder and leader at the House of Heart, a group home for women 45-60, struggling with mental illness and substance abuse, Nancy states that all of her accomplishments are attributed to her experience with her ill daughter, the greatest contributor to her life.